on

Cape Cod
and the Islands

A Naturalist's Hiking Guide

An Invitation to the Reader

If you find that conditions have changed along these walks, please let the author and publisher know so that corrections may be made in future printings. Address all correspondence to:

Editor
Walks and Rambles Series
Backcountry Publications
P.O. Box 748
Woodstock, VT 05091

Library of Congress Cataloging-in-Publication Data

Friary, Ned

    Walks & rambles on Cape Cod and the islands / Ned Friary and Glenda Bendure. — 2nd ed.

        p.   cm. — (Walks and rambles series)

    ISBN 0-88150-424-6 (alk. paper)

    1. Natural history—Massachusetts. 2. Nature Trails—Massachusetts—Cape Cod—Guidebooks. 3. Nature trails—Massachusetts—Martha's Vineyard—Guidebooks. 4. Nature trails—Massachusetts—Nantucket Island—Guidebooks. 5. Hiking—Massachusetts—Cape Cod—Guidebooks. 6. Hiking—Massachusetts—Martha's Vineyard—Guidebooks. 7. Hiking—Massachusetts—Nantucket Island—Guide-books. I. Bendure, Glenda. II. Title. III. Series: Walks & rambles guide.

QH105.M4F75 1998

508.755'9—dc21   98-13693

                                                      CIP

Published by Backcountry Publications
A division of The Countryman Press
PO Box 748, Woodstock, Vermont 05091
Distributed by W.W. Norton and Company
500 Fifth Avenue, New York, NY 10110

Design by Sally Sherman
Maps by Alex Wallach and Jacques Chazaud, © 1999 The Countryman Press
Cover photograph by Kimberly Grant
Interior photographs by Ned Friary
Printed in Canada
10 9 8 7 6 5 4 3 2 1

on

Cape Cod and the Islands

A Naturalist's Hiking Guide

SECOND EDITION

NED FRIARY AND GLENDA BENDURE

Backcountry Publications
Woodstock, Vermont

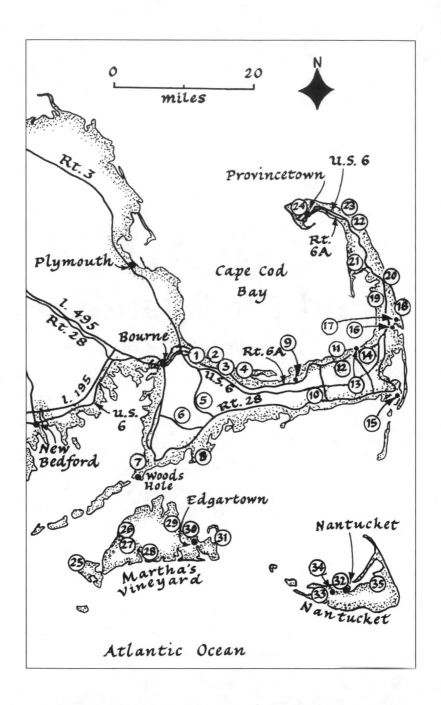

Contents

MARTHA'S VINEYARD

NANTUCKET

Acknowledgments

We would like to thank the following people who took time to share insights, answer questions, and provide assistance in numerous ways during this project: Robert Prescott, director of the Wellfleet Bay Wildlife Sanctuary; Peter Trull, naturalist at the Center for Coastal Studies; Woody Mills, director of the Ashumet Holly and Wildlife Sanctuary; Mary Beers, naturalist at the Green Briar Nature Center; Christine Gault, at the Waquoit Bay National Estuarine Research Reserve; Alison Robb, who leads nature walks for the Waquoit Bay National Estuarine Research Reserve; Chris Kennedy, Islands regional supervisor of the Trustees of Reservations; Tom Chase, refuge manager at Long Point Wildlife Refuge; Lisa McFadden, from the administrative office of the Trustees of Reservations; Dick Johnson, executive director of the Sheriff's Meadow Foundation; James Lengyel, executive director of the Martha's Vineyard Land Bank Commission; Gus Ben David, director of the Felix Neck Wildlife Sanctuary; Craig Hunter, at the Nantucket Land Bank; the staff at the Nantucket Conservation Foundation; and numerous rangers at the Cape Cod National Seashore, town conservation lands, and state parks.

Introduction

Cape Cod and the islands of Martha's Vineyard and Nantucket boast scores of scenic trails and pristine beaches that are ideal for leisurely walks and rambles. Nature lovers can explore varied woodlands, salt marshes, ocean shorelines, heathlands, freshwater ponds, cedar swamps, and tidal flats.

The beauty and serenity of the Cape and Islands have long attracted hikers, birders, and naturalists. Henry David Thoreau kept journals of his long walks on the Cape. Published in 1865 as *Cape Cod*, they alerted the world to the beauty of the lonely beaches along "the bared and bended arm of Massachusetts." Thoreau favored the long stretch of Outer Beach from Eastham to the tip of Provincetown. "A man may stand there," he said, "and put all America behind him."

Nearly a century later, photographs of a barefoot John F. Kennedy walking the beaches of his Cape Cod home touched the public consciousness. Thanks to the late president, much of the land Thoreau walked is today within the bounds of the Cape Cod National Seashore and remains as unspoiled as it was a hundred years ago.

The 1961 founding of the National Seashore, which set aside the majority of the Lower Cape as parklands, inspired a broad-based conservation movement to protect the Cape and Islands' fragile ecology. Since then, Cape Cod's municipal governments and more than a dozen private land trusts have acquired thousands of acres of land for the preservation of open space and environmentally sensitive habitats. In the mid-1980s, Nantucket and Martha's Vineyard took the unprecedented step of adding a 2 percent "land bank" tax on real estate transactions, generating funds for the purchase of conservation lands. All this effort has served not only to preserve vast tracts of unspoiled land on the Cape and Islands but also to open up many new areas for hikers and naturalists to explore.

Of the 35 hikes in this book, 31 are on parklands, public beaches, or other conservation areas. These include eight trails in the

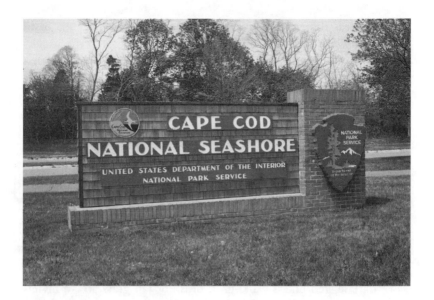

Cape Cod National Seashore as well as walks in a national wildlife refuge, two state parks, three Massachusetts Audubon Society sanctuaries, and a number of newly acquired town conservation properties.

We also include four walking tours of historic towns: Sandwich, Cape Cod's oldest town; Woods Hole, internationally renowned as a marine research center; and the well-preserved former whaling towns of Nantucket and Edgartown.

For a listing of conservation groups active in the preservation of natural spaces on Cape Cod and the Islands, see the appendix at the back of this book.

Walking the trails

Walking distances given at the beginning of each hike are round-trip unless otherwise noted. Walking times are an estimate of the time it takes to walk each route at a leisurely pace, allowing time to stop and enjoy viewpoints and other sights along the way. Hikers who prefer to walk briskly will undoubtedly be able to walk the trails in less time, whereas those who want to examine the flora and fauna or to linger in town museums will need to add more time onto the walks.

The Cape and Islands have excellent four-season hiking. With a climate tempered by the ocean, it's generally cooler in summer and warmer in winter than in inland areas. In spring, wildflowers bloom, and migrating birds stop off on their way north. Summer provides the opportunity for combining hiking with swimming. Fall lingers longer here than elsewhere in New England and is a delightful time for hiking, while winter offers solitude and crisp, blue skies.

During the warmer months, hikers should take precautions to protect themselves against ticks and poison ivy. Deer ticks, which are barely the size of a pinhead, can transmit Lyme disease—a serious malady that is long lived and potentially debilitating—as well as babesiosis, a malaria-like infection. Deer ticks are found anywhere there are white-tailed deer, though mice are also common carriers.

Bare-legged hikers walking in brush or tall grass are an invitation to ticks, which wait in low foliage until attracted by the heat and gases emitted by passing mammals. Local health officials recommend wearing light clothing on which the ticks can be easily spotted, wearing pants tucked into socks when walking through tall grass or brush, and avoiding deer trails. Always inspect for ticks carefully after finishing your walks.

Poison ivy abounds on the Cape and Islands as a viney shrub that climbs trees and grows along the ground among weeds and low bushes. Learn to identify its glossy, three-leaf configuration, and, when in doubt, remember: "Leaves of three, let it be."

Periodically, storms wrack the Cape and Islands and, in the process, alter the coastline. Typical beach erosion averages 1–3 feet annually, but hurricanes and unusually powerful storms have been known to cause as much as 40 feet of erosion from the face of some local beaches. Although some of the sands eventually return to the same beaches, others wash up elsewhere, in a process that's constantly reshaping and molding our shoreline. Because of these natural forces, hikers may sometimes find that beach accesses have been slightly modified or boardwalks rerouted, although all the trails in this book should be here far into the future.

Cape Cod, Martha's Vineyard, and Nantucket are wonderful places to explore. We hope this guide serves to introduce both visitors and residents to some of the Cape and Islands' special places.

Map symbols

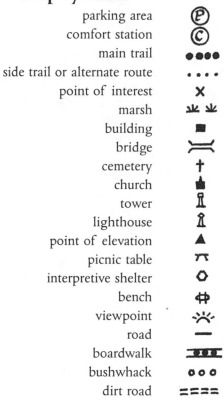

parking area	
comfort station	
main trail	
side trail or alternate route	
point of interest	
marsh	
building	
bridge	
cemetery	
church	
tower	
lighthouse	
point of elevation	
picnic table	
interpretive shelter	
bench	
viewpoint	
road	
boardwalk	
bushwhack	
dirt road	

Cape Cod

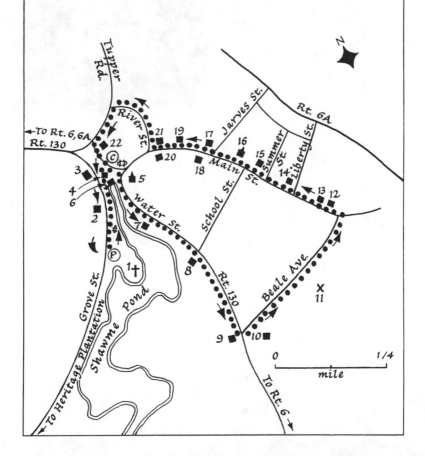

Sandwich Village

A walking tour around Shawme Pond and the historic district of the Cape's oldest town

Hiking distance: 1¼ miles
Hiking time: 1½ hours

Sandwich, the first permanent English settlement on Cape Cod, was incorporated in 1639. It is Cape Cod's oldest town.

Records of Plymouth Colony from 1637 state that the court allowed Sandwich to be settled by "tenn men of Saugust" (from Saugus Plantation, the present-day town of Lynn), who "shall have liberty to view a place to sitt down & have sufficient lands for three score famylies."

Now, as then, the village center is along Main Street and around Shawme Pond. It's a quiet area of small museums, historic sites, and scenes of natural beauty. Children will be especially fascinated by the ducks, geese, and swans that make the pond their home.

Even in summer, the historic district of Sandwich is devoid of the hustle and bustle and the commercialism that mark many of the larger towns on Cape Cod. Thanks to protective zoning in the village center, shops are discreet, and historic homes are intact. In fact, many of the shops along the walk are housed within restored period homes, offering opportunities to see some of their lovely interiors.

Sandwich is a fine walking town year-round, although many of its attractions are closed during the winter.

Access

Sandwich's historic district is just off Route 6A and can be reached by turning south on Route 130, on Tupper Road, or on Main Street. You can also take exit 2 from Route 6 and drive 1 mile north on Route 130.

We begin this walking tour at the Old Town Cemetery on Grove Street. There's space to park in front of the cemetery, off the side of the road. You can begin the walk just as easily, however, from any other point along the way. Parking is available along Main Street and near the Burgess Museum on Water Street. Hoxie House and the glass museum have parking for their patrons.

Trail

The walk starts at Old Town Cemetery, where members of the town's founding families—Bourne, Bodfish, Burgess, and others—are laid to rest. The graveyard is on a small neck of land that juts out into Shawme Pond, offering a nice view of the water. Many of the older, lichen-encrusted gravestones are decorated with the carving of a winged skull, a common Puritan design. The human skull served as a reminder of the fate that awaits the living, while the wings suggested resurrection. The oldest marker dates back to 1683 (Thomas Clark), and numerous others are from the 1700s.

From the cemetery, walk north toward the center of town and you'll soon come to a couple of pond-side benches. This spot is a favorite for local children who come here to look at the many water birds that live on Shawme Pond. In spring and summer, fluffy ducklings, goslings, and cygnets swim alongside their mothers.

The two-story Colonial house across the street has a plaque marking it as the former home of Peter Newcomb. Built in 1703, it was the first tavern in Sandwich, with rooms for overnight guests. During the turmoil of the Revolution, Newcomb Tavern served as a meeting place for British loyalists.

Descended from the original one-room homes of the earliest settlers, Colonial-style houses are distinguishable by their huge central fireplaces, which served as the heating source for the entire dwelling. Colonial houses are also characterized by simple lines and an absence of ornamentation.

The old Newcomb Tavern is just the first of many houses along the route marked by small date plates showing the year of construction. Interestingly, some houses have two plates—one with the construction date of the original building and another for a later addition. Cape Codders were noted for enlarging their homes as new generations came along.

The grand Federal-style home at the corner of Main and Grove Streets now houses H. Richard Strand Antiques. Inside you'll find museum-quality displays of furniture, dishes, glassware, and items from the China trade similar to those that might have been in the homes of wealthy New Englanders from about 1750 to 1850. The house itself was built in the early 1800s by Seth Freeman Nye, a leading lawyer and one of the richest men in Sandwich. It is said that Seth Nye never charged his clients more than $9.99—even if he had to send several bills of that amount—because taxes were levied on bills of $10.00 or more!

On the traffic island where Grove Street, Tupper Road, and Route 130 come together, there's a tall monument dedicated to veterans of the Civil War, flanked by two large Norway spruce trees.

The large white building on the corner is Sandwich Town Hall. Distinguished by its tall Doric columns, it was built in 1834 to replace a smaller meeting hall and continues to hold the town's public offices. You might notice people lining up to fill water jugs at the fountain on the side of Town Hall. The water rises freely from an artesian well, and here you can get a drink of what many residents claim is the best water on Cape Cod. Across the street is a small park with rest rooms, a pay phone, a bench, and a pretty view of the brook that flows out of Shawme Pond.

Perched above the village, the First Church of Christ (circa 1847) sits on a knoll at the corner of Main and Water Streets. It's a classic New England Congregational church, noted for its graceful spire built in the Christopher Wren style. Inside the church is a brass bell that was cast in 1675 and is believed to be the oldest church bell in America. The bell was a gift to the town by the widow of Captain Peter Adolph. The captain, who was shipwrecked and washed ashore in Sandwich in 1702, is buried in Old Town Cemetery.

The picturesque Dexter Grist Mill, around the corner from Town Hall, has been restored as a working 17th-century mill, complete with a wooden waterwheel. The mill was built in 1646 to grind grain for the early settlers. During the summer, visitors can watch corn being ground into cornmeal and can even buy a bag to take home. There is a small admission fee.

Continue your hike down Water Street, where you'll soon come to the Thornton W. Burgess Museum on the shores of Shawme Pond. This museum commemorates the Sandwich author and naturalist who wrote 170 books in the early 1900s. Most were children's stories, with characters such as Reddy Fox and Peter Rabbit. Burgess used actual sites in Sandwich as settings for many of his animal adventures. Inside the small museum are displays of Burgess's works; drawings by Harrison Cady, who illustrated most of the stories; and a gift shop. Admission is by donation.

A little farther along Water Street is the Hoxie House, the oldest house on Cape Cod. Built in 1675 of saltbox construction, this handsome house has a steeply sloped, north-facing roof and small leaded windows, features that help ward off the chilling winter winds that whip in from the north. The house is named for Abraham Hoxie, a whaling captain who resided here in the 1800s. In the 1950s, the town purchased the house from the captain's descendants and restored the site. Inside are chamfered beams, a huge open hearth, and furnishings of the early colonial period. The small admission charge includes a guided tour.

If your time is limited, you could now shorten this walking tour by heading down School Street and then turning left on Main Street. Otherwise, continue south on Water Street to Quail Hollow Farm store, which is housed in a quaint New England barn (circa 1840). Inside, the fruits and vegetables are arranged in picture-perfect displays. Quail Hollow also sells fresh-baked goods and locally made pickles, vinegars, and preserves, including beach plum jelly, a traditional Cape Cod spread.

Next, turn left down Beale Avenue past Henry T. Wing School. The bandstand behind the school is the site of free concerts performed by the Sandwich Town Band on summer evenings.

At the end of Beale Avenue, turn left on Main Street. You'll first pass a couple of homes built in 1774 and 1775 and then come

The swans of Shawme Pond and the Dexter Grist Mill are elements of a quintessential New England village scene.

to the Masonic Hall, housed in the former Methodist church (1847), and St. John's Episcopal Church (1899), with its dark shingles and bright red door.

Main Street has a collection of antiques shops, art galleries, gift shops, and bed & breakfast inns. Many of these establishments, such as Home for the Holidays Gifts, Isaiah Jones Homestead, and Capt. Ezra Nye House, are in beautifully restored historic homes. Brown Jug Antiques, at the corner of Main and Jarves Streets, has a nicely displayed collection of Sandwich glass that's particularly worth a look if you're not planning to visit the glass museum.

Just down the road is the Dan'l Webster Inn, the largest hotel and restaurant in the village. The original tavern and inn opened in the mid-1700s and was a gathering place for Patriots during the Revolution. For years it kept a room reserved for Daniel Webster, who frequently came to Sandwich to fish and to hunt deer. Although the current building looks like it dates back to the colonial period, it was actually built in 1973, two years after the old inn burned down.

A little farther on is Yesteryears Doll Museum, which has an extensive collection of antique dolls, dollhouses, and miniatures, plus a shop for collectors. The museum is housed in the old steepled First Parish Church, said to be the only church building in town with stained-glass windows made of original Sandwich glass. Admission is charged.

From here, turn right on River Street and follow it around to Tupper Road for a walk past a scenic marsh. Then turn left on Tupper Road to get to the Sandwich Glass Museum.

In 1825, the Boston and Sandwich Glass Company opened the first glassmaking factory in Sandwich. The industry flourished and brought prosperity to the town. "Sandwich glass" had become a household term by the middle of the 19th century and remains well known among glass collectors today. The term refers to all forms of blown and pressed glassware made in Sandwich.

Sandwich Glass Museum exhibits an excellent collection of lacy pressed glass from the 1830s. Other displays include blown glassware with fine engravings, elaborately designed candlesticks, oil lamps, and paperweights. The museum also tells the story of the town's glass-making history—which ended with a labor strike in 1888—and has a small display of antique furniture, artifacts, and interesting period photographs. There is a modest admission charge.

From the museum, cross Route 130 and walk south on Grove Street. This will bring you back to the cemetery and to the end of our walking tour.

If you have a few extra hours, you might drive (or walk) ½ mile south on Grove Street to Heritage Plantation of Sandwich. Heritage Plantation features nature paths that wind through landscaped gardens and along the shore of Upper Shawme Pond. Hundreds of Dexter rhododendron bushes, hybridized at this site by Charles O. Dexter, bloom from mid-May through mid-June. Heritage Plantation also has American folk art and history exhibits, a windmill, a working 1912 carousel, and an exceptional antique car collection housed in a reproduction of a classic Shaker round barn. It's open from Mother's Day through mid-October, and admission is charged. There's a picnic area outside the grounds.

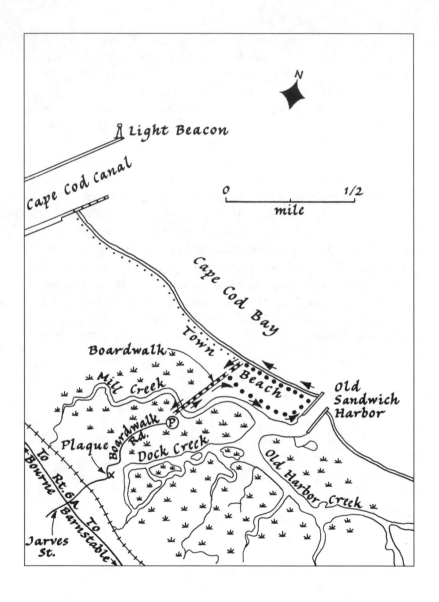

Sandwich Boardwalk and Town Beach

A boardwalk across a scenic marsh to an Upper Cape beach

Hiking distance: 1½ miles
Hiking time: 1 hour

This easy walk starts on a long boardwalk that crosses Mill Creek and the expansive Town Neck Marsh, then loops along the edge of the marsh to Old Sandwich Harbor and Cape Cod Bay. We've walked this route many times, in every season and even at night under a full moon, and it's always a pleasant walk. In early summer, the marsh grasses are lush and green; in August and September, the fragile sprays of sea lavender bloom; and in late autumn, the glasswort turns red and the marsh grasses golden.

The Boston and Sandwich Glass Company, the earliest and most prestigious of Sandwich's famous glass companies, built its factory on the edge of Town Neck Marsh in 1825 (a plaque at the end of Factory Street marks the spot). The company took good advantage of its marsh-side location. The salt-marsh hay was cut and harvested to use as soft packing material for boxes of glassware, which were then shipped by small boat down the marsh waterways and out Sandwich Harbor.

The impressive 1,350-foot-long boardwalk that stands above the marsh and crosses Mill Creek was first constructed in 1875 to provide Sandwich residents easy access to Town Beach. Battered by severe winter storms and the occasional hurricane, it has been rebuilt many times since. The current boardwalk dates to 1992 and was funded and built entirely by volunteers. As you walk along it, you'll notice names engraved onto each of the 1,600 planks, acknowledging those who contributed to the reconstruction. Because of mushy

Though rebuilt many times, the Sandwich Boardwalk has spanned Mill Creek for more than a hundred years.

marsh mud and periodic frost heaves, the boards are never completely level, but this tipsy effect is part of its charm.

Town Beach, at the end of the boardwalk, does have some patches of soft white sand, but the beach is covered predominantly by pebbles that crunch underfoot and give your leg muscles a healthy workout. The tide washes the pebbles up on the shoreline and often sorts them according to size. The rows of tiny pebbles, small pebbles, medium pebbles, and larger stones look just like a gravel yard with all the sample sizes spread out on display.

We see something different each time we walk this beach. One time, scores of pink starfish had been washed up on shore; another time we saw hundreds of empty sea urchin shells, some with their short green spines still attached; at other times there were periwinkles in such quantity they could be scooped up by the handful.

Access

As you come into Sandwich Village from Bourne, take Route 6A. In Sandwich, at the village's only traffic light, turn left off Route 6A and onto Jarves Street. Cross the railroad tracks and go straight, turning left on Factory Street and then right on Boardwalk Road. Boardwalk Road ends at a parking area at the start of the boardwalk, 0.8 mile north of Route 6A.

Trail

The first ¼ mile of the trail is on the boardwalk over Town Neck Marsh. After a few hundred feet, the boardwalk passes over the meandering waters of Mill Creek. These waters, which ebb and flow with the tides, nourish the salt marsh and provide a nursery for many ocean fish, including the striped bass prized by fishermen. Schools of minnows dart about in the creek and in the narrow marsh channels that run beside the boardwalk. From May to October, terns can often be spotted gliding over the marsh, dive-bombing for these small fish and for insects.

Marshes are breeding grounds for many insects, including the pesky greenhead fly that is prevalent on Cape Cod's north-side beaches in late summer. The blue wooden boxes placed about the marsh are greenhead fly traps. Great blue herons, green herons, snowy egrets, and yellowlegs (a long-legged sandpiper) all feed in the marsh. The wooden platform on the east side of the marsh is an osprey nesting post.

As you come to the end of the marsh, you'll notice what might appear to be unusually uniform sand dunes. These dunes were created by bulldozers in the winter of 1991, using sand dredged from the Cape Cod Canal, in an effort to protect the salt marsh from the destructive blasts of winter storms. American beach grass has been planted in neat rows to stabilize the sand and keep the dunes from blowing away.

Rather than continuing on the last section of the boardwalk that has been built over these new dunes, turn right onto the trail that skirts the marsh flats and follows Mill Creek.

After ⅓ mile, Mill Creek widens, at which point Dock Creek and Old Harbor Creek join in and the creeks flow together out through Old Sandwich Harbor and into the bay. In the 1800s, all three creeks had wharves along them, and boat and barge traffic moved up these narrow waterways carrying goods right into the heart of Sandwich. The trail leads up from the marsh to Town Beach, where a seawall lines the narrow mouth of Old Sandwich Harbor.

From here, it's a straight walk down the beach back to the boardwalk, about 15 minutes away. As you walk down the beach, you'll be looking toward the east entrance of Cape Cod Canal, marked by a long stone jetty with a light beacon at its tip. The construction of Cape Cod Canal, the world's widest sea-level canal, effectively turned Cape Cod from a peninsula into an island. The canal has been a boon to ships making the Boston–New York run, cutting a hundred miles off the route and allowing them to avoid the shoals and treacherous waters of the Outer Cape, which have claimed hundreds of ships over the years. In the 30 years before the canal's completion in 1914, for instance, more than a hundred lives were lost in ships that went down after striking the sandy shoals off the tips of Provincetown and Chatham.

During the height of the summer, hundreds of ships pass through the Cape Cod Canal each day—private yachts and sailboats, cruise liners, fishing boats, oil tankers, and tow barges. The current shifts direction four times a day, flowing from Cape Cod Bay to Buzzards Bay and then back again.

If you'd like to take a closer look at Cape Cod Canal, you can extend this walk by continuing down the beach to its end and walking out onto the huge stone jetty at the entrance of the canal. The round trip to the canal along the beach from the boardwalk is about 2½ miles and takes about 1½ hours to walk.

Murkwood Conservation Lands

An easy woodland walk offering scenic marsh views

Hiking distance: 1¼ miles
Hiking time: 45 minutes

The Sandwich Conservation Commission's 79-acre Murkwood property is an old farmstead that extends deep into Scorton Marsh. The trail winds through a diverse woodland, skirting the marsh in a number of places to provide some very scenic views.

The Murkwood property was acquired by the town of Sandwich in 1978. The trails are level, easy, and well maintained, but the ground can be quite wet in springtime and after heavy rains, especially on the western side of the acreage. There is also an abundance of poison ivy in the woods.

Although the trail winds amidst a wide variety of trees and shrubs, a special feature is the groves of eastern red cedar at the north side of the property. The woodlands provide habitat for numerous birds, including blue jays, woodpeckers, woodcocks, and crows. The golden-crowned kinglet, a beautiful little bird with a bright yellow crown and a high-pitched chirp, flocks here with chickadees and tufted titmice in fall and winter.

One of the interesting wildflowers found along the trail is the rare Indian cucumber, with its double whorls of leaves and small, greenish yellow flowers, which grows in the rich soil amongst the cedars. Another flower found in the woodlands is the trout lily (also known as dogtooth violet), a small yellow lily with large, mottled leaves. The trout lily blooms in early spring; the Indian cucumber, from midspring to early summer.

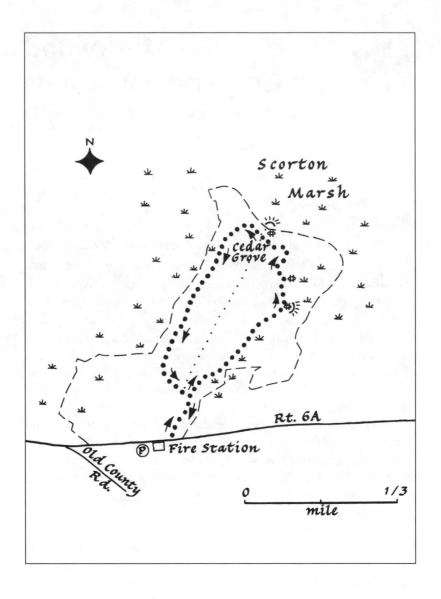

Spring wildflowers decorate the woodland floor along the Murkwood Trail.

Access

The trailhead is on Route 6A in East Sandwich. Parking for the trail is provided at the west side of the East Sandwich fire station on Route 6A, which is 0.4 mile east of Christy's Colonial Market and 2.3 miles west of the Sandwich/Barnstable town line. From the fire station, walk 100 yards east to get to the trailhead, which begins on the north side of Route 6A. This is a busy road; use caution when crossing.

Trail

The trail begins at the left side of the MURKWOOD CONSERVATION LANDS sign in a woods of oak and tupelo trees. You'll soon enter a section of sassafras, easy to identify by its mitten-shaped leaves and thin, twisting trunks. The leaves and stems of sassafras are spicy and aromatic, and the roots have traditionally been used to make tea.

In a couple of minutes, the trail forks. Bear right, and a few minutes later you'll briefly skirt the marsh for a tease of a view. The trail then turns inland, passes some white birch trees, and comes back out to the edge of a clearing where marsh-side benches beckon from beneath a small stand of tupelo. This spot is a good vantage point for observing the birdlife in the marsh, and, with a little luck, you might spot herons, a circling marsh hawk, or even an osprey.

The trail continues by winding through a thicket of eastern red cedar before coming to another marsh-side bench. Continue through the woods, and after a few minutes you'll come to a path on the left that runs directly back through the woods to the trailhead. Ignore this trail and, instead, continue ahead, bearing to the right. You'll immediately come to a little spur trail that leads about 50 yards out to a scenic perch at the edge of the marsh. From here, there's a wonderful, clear view across Scorton Marsh to the distant, shingled cottages that line East Sandwich Beach. To your right, the meandering Scorton Creek cuts through the marsh and empties into Scorton Harbor on Cape Cod Bay. Also visible to your right is an upland marsh island that's high enough to stay dry during high tides, allowing trees to take root on it.

When you're ready to leave, walk back out to the main trail and continue to the right. You'll pass through a pleasant grove of maple and cedar trees before the trail comes out along the west side of the marsh. The trail continues through a section of holly trees, completes the loop, and brings you back out to Route 6A.

Sandy Neck

A hearty hike down the beach, through sand dunes, and back along a marsh

Hiking distance: 4¾ miles
Hiking time: 2½ hours

Sandy Neck is a 6¼-mile-long barrier beach separating Barnstable Harbor and the Great Marshes from Cape Cod Bay. The Sandy Neck peninsula, which varies in width from a few hundred yards to half a mile, has built up over the past three thousand years as sand eroded elsewhere on the Cape has been deposited here by longshore currents. Over time, the beach sand has been picked up by the wind and blown inland, where it has formed expansive dunes reaching heights of 50–100 feet.

One of five major dune systems on Cape Cod, Sandy Neck has not only primary sand dunes, which are common on many beaches, but also a well-established secondary dune system. Many of these inland dunes have stabilized and are covered with beach grasses, wildflowers, wild cranberries, and other vegetation. The oldest of the dunes have well-developed soils that support hardwood forests, including stands of coastal basswood and American holly.

Sandy Neck is one of the most dynamic and complex ecosystems on the Cape and was the first place in Massachusetts to be designated an Area of Critical Environmental Concern under the Wetlands Protection Act. The dunes provide a habitat for several endangered species, including piping plovers, which nest on the high beach; diamond-back terrapins, turtles that live in salt marsh but lay their eggs in the dunes; and eastern spadefoot toads, which breed in the dune bogs.

Indians set up summertime encampments on Sandy Neck, and the numerous midden piles they left are periodically uncovered by the

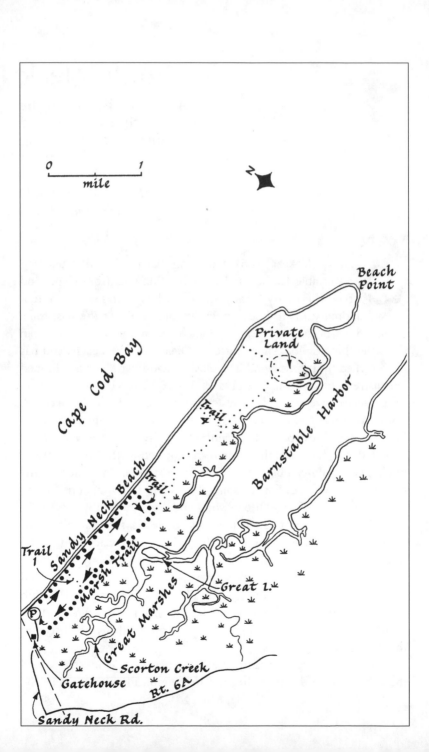

shifting sands. Arrowheads, hearthstones, flint chips, and tools have all been excavated from former campsites. In 1644, European colonists purchased the land from the Indians for three axes and four coats. The white settlers used the salt marsh as hayfields, and, in the 18th century, Sandy Neck was the site of a tryworks, where whale blubber was rendered for its oil. In the mid-1800s, commercial cranberry operations were begun on Sandy Neck, with nearly one hundred bogs placed under cultivation, a venture that continued until the early 1940s. During World War II, the military used the dunes as a training ground for troops destined for battles in the Sahara.

There are now about 50 rustic summer cottages at Sandy Neck. Although some are solitary cabins scattered about, most are part of a summer community at the tip of the peninsula known as Beach Point. Some of the buildings on Beach Point are listed on the National Register of Historic Places, including the decommissioned 19th-century Sandy Neck Light and the lightkeeper's quarters, now privately owned.

Sandy Neck is managed for both conservation and multi-use recreation. During the summer, it is the Upper Cape's most popular north-side bathing beach. It is also well used for surf fishing, shellfishing, and seasonal hunting.

Although Sandy Neck is a good place to hike year-round, summer has some disadvantages. Not only can the unshaded trails make for hot walking, but also the beach is busy with over-sand vehicles plying up and down. In winter, the walk offers solitude, but pick a calm day since north winds can blow cold and gusty off the bay.

Access

From Route 6A in East Sandwich, turn north onto Sandy Neck Road 2 miles east of the East Sandwich fire station or 0.2 mile west of the Barnstable/Sandwich town line. Sandy Neck Road leads 1¼ miles directly into the beach parking lot. From Memorial Day to Labor Day, daily parking fees are charged ($10 at this writing) for all vehicles except those with beach stickers from the towns of Sandwich or Barnstable. For more information, call the gatehouse at 508-362-8306.

Note that the Marsh Trail can have muddy conditions at any time, and sections are sometimes flooded during high tide; inquire at the gatehouse for current conditions. Hikers are not allowed to enter areas marked EROSION CONTROL or PRIVATE PROPERTY, and they should stay on established trails while in the interior dunes.

Trail

We start the hike along the beach, cross the dunes on Trail #2, and come back along the marsh—a 4¾-mile hike. You could, instead, cross the dunes at Trail #4 and make this a 9-mile hike, or walk all the way down to the tip of Sandy Neck and back before taking Trail #4, turning it into a 13-mile, all-day hike.

From the parking lot, wooden stairs lead down to the beach. In recent years, winter storms have undermined the coastal dunes here, causing about a third of the parking lot to wash into the sea—a vivid example of how the winds and tides are constantly reshaping Sandy Neck's shoreline.

At the bottom of the stairs, turn right and walk east along the beach for about 2 miles. Sandy Neck's character changes with the season. Generally, most of the beach is sandy in summer and fall and scattered with smooth stones in winter and spring, both conditions fine for walking. The beach is backed by low sand dunes laced with American beach grass, a native plant that stabilizes the dunes. Sandy Neck looks out onto the open waters of Cape Cod Bay, and when it's clear, you can see the coastline of Plymouth County to the northwest, the Lower Cape to the northeast.

Along the shoreline, sandpipers dart back and forth chasing the outgoing waves, plucking up mole crabs and tiny marine creatures that wash up onto the beach. You'll notice that some of the dunes are fenced off to protect another shorebird, the piping plover, which breeds on Sandy Neck from April through August. Piping plovers nest on wide, open beaches, laying their eggs in a simple depression in the sand. They are vulnerable to predators, such as the foxes, skunks, and raccoons that roam Sandy Neck at night, and to human feet and vehicle tires that can accidentally crush the camouflaged eggs and sand-colored chicks.

The decommissioned 19th-century Sandy Neck Light and the former lightkeeper's quarters mark the eastern end of Sandy Neck.

After walking about 45 minutes down the beach from the parking lot, look closely for a sign between two low dunes on the upper beach marking Trail #2. Turn right onto this trail for a 10-minute hike through soft sands to the marsh. Fragrant bayberry bushes, dusty miller, and seaside goldenrod are common alongside the path. This is also a good place to identify the tracks of animals that inhabit the dunes and marsh. Foxes leave distinctive, close-stepped tracks, all in a line, resembling that of a cat, whereas the hooves of white-tailed deer leave heavily indented trails running up and down the face of the dunes.

Notice as you walk across the dunes that they tend to be sharper and steeper on the windward north side and more gently sloping on the leeward marsh side. Along the trail, you'll pass a small, weathered, private cottage, and around the bend on the right, the remains of an old brick chimney being buried by shifting sands.

When Trail #2 comes out to the marsh, turn right and proceed along the Marsh Trail, which runs between the Great Marshes and the back side of the Sandy Neck dunes. This section of the trail offers superlative views of the expansive, unspoiled marsh and the meandering waters of Scorton Creek.

The Great Marshes provides habitat for a wide variety of plant and animal life. Look for great blue herons standing majestically in the marsh, northern harriers gliding over the grasses in search of rodents, and the occasional osprey. Partway down the trail, you'll pass Great Island, a wooded marsh island that shelters yellow warblers and other songbirds.

Although the Marsh Trail is a beautiful walk in any season, it's particularly lovely in early fall when the greens and golds of the marsh grasses are highlighted by the red sheen of slender glasswort and the pale purple patches of sea lavender. Migrating monarch butterflies are drawn by fall-blooming asters, and bright yellow goldenrod adorns the dunes.

After about an hour's walk, the Marsh Trail ends at Sandy Neck Road, and from there it's ¼ mile back along the vehicle road to the beach parking lot.

Lowell Holly Reservation

A woodland walk through beeches and hollies, with pond views

Hiking distance: 2¾ miles
Hiking time: 1½ hours

Lowell Holly Reservation, a property of the Trustees of Reservations, is an unspoiled woodland preserve of American beech and American holly trees. The property was bequeathed to the conservation organization in 1943 by Abbott Lawrence Lowell, a former president of Harvard University. The Trustees of Reservations was, incidentally, founded in 1891 by Charles Eliot, the son of an earlier Harvard president.

Lowell Holly Reservation is on Conaumet Neck, the 130-acre peninsula that divides two of Cape Cod's largest freshwater ponds— Wakeby Pond to the north and Mashpee Pond to the south. The ponds are a popular recreational site, offering sandy beaches and good swimming, canoeing, and trout fishing.

Although the reservation takes its name from the more than three hundred hollies on the property, the most dominant tree here is the American beech, a sturdy tree whose silvery gray bark and light-colored leaves add a nice, bright touch to the woods. This is one of the largest native beech forests remaining on the Cape, having been virtually untouched for the past 200 years.

Among the many native wildflowers you can find along the trail are pink lady's slipper, a spring-blooming orchid; silverrod, a slender member of the goldenrod family with silvery flower heads; and beechdrops, a branching, brownish, parasitic plant that lives under beech trees.

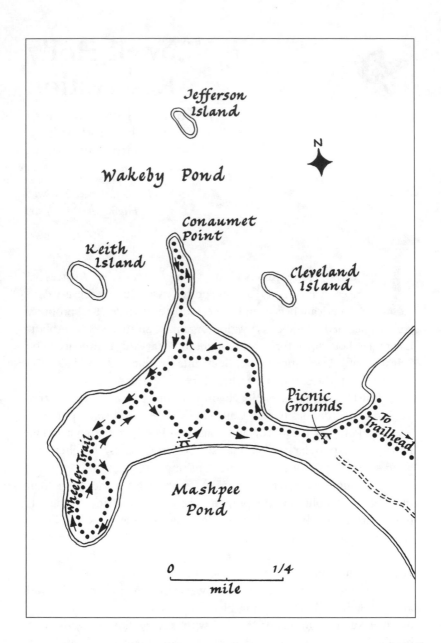

A lone fisherman enjoys the serenity of Wakeby Pond, as seen through the branches of an American beech tree.

This is an easy woodland walk, although lowland sections of the trail can get muddy in the spring and after periods of heavy rain.

Access

Lowell Holly Reservation is in the town of Mashpee, near the Mashpee/Sandwich town line. From Route 6, take exit 2 and follow Route 130 south 1.5 miles. Turn left onto Cotuit Road and go 3.4 miles, turning right onto South Sandwich Road. Continue for 0.6 mile, and then turn right into a small roadside parking lot at the trailhead.

Trail

The trail, which begins at the west side of the parking lot, passes through a pleasant, rolling woods of pine, oak, and beech trees. After about 15 minutes, you'll reach Wakeby Pond, where you turn left for a short shoreline walk to the picnic grounds. There you'll find magnificent holly trees, picnic tables with pond views, and a grand old sprawling beech tree at the water's edge.

The trail continues at the left side of the picnic grounds and leads across a narrow neck to the main body of the peninsula. At its narrowest point, the neck is almost cut by the ponds, with a swampy area just a few feet off the left side of the trail and Wakeby Pond to the right. It takes just two minutes to cross the neck, where the trail immediately forks. Take the narrower trail to the right, which follows above the perimeter of Wakeby Pond.

Beside the path, a variety of ferns and mosses grow, as does pipsissewa, a wintergreen with white-streaked, deep green leaves, and Indian pipe, a translucent white plant with a nodding flower that pops up like a mushroom in summer. A scattering of hollies and rhododendrons in the surrounding woods adds a nice green touch in all seasons. The majority of the reservation's many rhododendrons are of the Catawba variety, which has bright pink, 2-inch flowers that bloom in May.

After a few minutes, the trail skirts the edge of the pond, where it passes some red maple trees, then proceeds up a hill through a beech woods and back down along a swamp before reaching another hill. There, the trail turns inland over springy peat and passes a large mass of rhododendrons as it winds up the hill. At the top, the trail veers left and shortly comes to a T-junction.

Turn right at the junction for a 10-minute walk across a narrow spit of land to Conaumet Point. This trail, marked with white square blazes, passes through a woods of beech, oaks, and hollies, with blueberry and huckleberry along the damper lowland sections. At the point, there's a view of the three islands in Wakeby Pond: from left to right, Keith Island, Jefferson Island, and Cleveland Island.

Upon returning from Conaumet Point, continue straight ahead on the main trail, passing the route you entered on. Here the trail becomes wider, as it marks the start of the old carriage road used by Dr. Lowell.

In less than 5 minutes, you'll reach a fork. The wider left path continues the circle route back to the trailhead, while the path on the right begins the 30-minute Wheeler Trail. Turn right onto this lollipop-shaped side trail, which is marked with white square blazes and is named for Wilfrid Wheeler, Lowell Holly Reservation's first chairman. Wheeler, who added 50 heavily fruiting holly trees to the native hollies already on the grounds, wanted to develop the reservation as a place to study the American holly, which approaches its northernmost range on Cape Cod.

The Wheeler Trail climbs up and down some mild hills, passing stands of white pines and pitch pines as well as some black birches and the ubiquitous beech trees. In less than 10 minutes, you'll reach a fork that marks the start of a loop. Take it in a clockwise direction, bearing left between two blazed beech trees. There are good views of Mashpee Pond before the trail reaches land's end and curves back around to finish the loop.

Continue back to the start of the Wheeler Trail, at the intersection with the old carriage road, and turn right. The trail passes some boggy areas and, in a few minutes, comes to a fork, where a short spur to the right leads down to a picnic table on a sandy beach. The trail to the left continues for a 10-minute walk through the woods back to the picnic grounds.

Should you wish to wander further, you can walk northeast from the picnic grounds along the shoreline to the adjacent Ryder Conservation Lands. This property, in the town of Sandwich, is crossed with a network of trails that skirt Wakeby Pond and pass through marshes, abandoned cranberry bogs, and mixed woodlands.

Ashumet Holly and Wildlife Sanctuary

A Massachusetts Audubon Society sanctuary with holly trees and good birding

Hiking distance: 1¼ miles
Hiking time: 1 hour

The 45-acre Ashumet Holly and Wildlife Sanctuary is a mix of woodlands and fields encircling a large freshwater pond. It is a special delight for nature lovers, who will find an abundance of birds and nearly one thousand holly trees.

The sanctuary's roots date back to the 1920s, when Wilfrid Wheeler, the first commissioner of agriculture in Massachusetts, began transplanting and propagating holly trees on the grounds. Wheeler undertook his conservation effort in response to the rapid decline of native hollies in the wild, the result of encroaching development and overzealous Christmastime harvesting.

Today, there are eight species and 65 varieties of American, Oriental, and European hollies at the sanctuary. Following Wheeler's death in 1961, the property was purchased by Josiah Lilly III, who gifted the preserve to the Massachusetts Audubon Society.

The banks of the sanctuary's Grassy Pond provide a habitat for rare wildflowers, including the thread-leaved sundew, an insectivorous plant whose sticky hairs act much like flypaper, and the Plymouth gentian, a pretty pink flower with a yellow center. Also on the grounds are a few franklinia, a member of the tea family that has large, solitary white flowers that bloom in fall. A native of the southeastern United States, this small tree vanished from the wild two hun-

dred years ago, just twenty years after it was first discovered, and now exists only in cultivation.

In addition to the sanctuary's unique flora, more than 130 bird species have been sighted at Ashumet, including more than 50 that nest on the grounds. The most prominent nesters are the barn swallows, which have returned to Ashumet each spring since 1935. The most common return date is April 18, though their arrival can vary by a week or two. The swallows move into the loft of the old barn at the property entrance, perform mating rituals, build mud-daub nests lined with feathers, and lay their eggs. By June, the barn is abuzz with activity, as hungry chicks twitter from the rafters and parents swoop back and forth snatching up flying insects to feed their young. When

A hiker pauses to look for birds along the trail in Ashumet.

the last fledglings are ready, usually in late August, the swallows depart on their long migration back to wintering grounds in Central and South America.

The sanctuary offers something for all seasons: wildflowers and rhododendrons in the spring, the nesting swallows and lush green growth of summer, franklinia blossoms in the fall, and the glossy green leaves and red berries of holly in winter.

Access

The sanctuary is on Ashumet Road in East Falmouth, on the north side of Route 151. Coming from the east, take Route 28 to the Mashpee Rotary. At the rotary, take Route 151 for 2.7 miles, then turn right onto Currier Road just past the Barnstable County Fairgrounds. Take the next right onto Ashumet Road and make an immediate left into the parking lot. If coming from North Falmouth, take Route 151 4 miles east from Route 28 and turn left onto Currier Road.

The trails are open every day from sunrise to sunset. Admission is free to Massachusetts Audubon Society members. Nonmember fees are $3 for adults, $2 for children under 15 and senior citizens 60 and older. Information about naturalist programs and guided walks may be obtained by calling the sanctuary at 508-563-6390.

Trail

Ashumet maintains a network of connecting trails, which we combine here to take in the highlights of the sanctuary. The trails are well defined, and the walking is easy.

The trailhead begins at the sanctuary parking lot, where hikers are commonly greeted with a wonderful orchestration of birdsong. From the back of the visitors center, a grassy trail leads north past a small field lined with birdhouses, which provide homes for nesting tree swallows. In autumn, look close to find a ground cover whose lustrous blue and purple berries look so much like porcelain beads it's called the porcelain berry vine. The fruit of this invasive exotic is eaten by robins, catbirds, cardinals, and mockingbirds.

A hundred feet beyond the field, turn left at the first junction.

The shrubs with distinctive black berries at the left side of the junction are Japanese holly. Holly berries are favored by a variety of birds, including bobwhites, bluebirds, hermit thrushes, and kingbirds.

In about 5 minutes, a trail comes in from the right; continue on the main trail, which bears left. The trail forks again after about 200 feet; here bear right, and almost immediately you'll come to a spur trail that leads down to the right. If you want a scenic detour, it's just 100 feet down this spur to a bench with a fine pond-side view. Otherwise, continue straight up the slope to the Wheeler Memorial, a small hilltop clearing surrounded by tall American holly trees, each a different variety. The holly directly in front of the bench is a 'Goldie', named for its unusual yellow-green berries. Beneath another holly tree is a plaque to Wilfrid Wheeler that commemorates his efforts in preserving the American holly.

From the memorial, the trail continues north along a windbreak of Norway spruce trees. Along this section of the trail, you'll find several varieties of English holly trees, recognizable by their leaves, which have a higher gloss than their American counterparts. English holly blossoms in May, a full month ahead of the American holly; thus, the two don't cross-pollinate.

Continue along the main trail for about ¼ mile, passing pines blazed with blue dots, until you reach a four-way intersection. Larger trails lead off to the left and right, but instead go straight ahead onto the narrow path that has been dubbed the Mystery Tree Trail for its unusual trees. Two distinctive species on the left side of the trail are the Japanese umbrella pine, whose needles form a fountain shape, and the cryptomeria, an attractive Japanese cedar with shaggy red bark.

This section of the trail ends after passing a unique, twin-trunked holly tree. The front of the tree, which is female, has prickly leaves and red berries, while the back of the tree is a berryless male with smooth leaves.

Just beyond the twin holly, turn right and follow the dirt road south about 100 feet, where you pick up the trail again on the right and head back into the woods and down to Grassy Pond. To take a short detour to see the fall-blooming franklinia, turn right on the path that intersects the trail about two-thirds of the way down to the pond. There's a franklinia about 100 yards down the path, on the north side.

The trail continues around the pond's east side. In summer, Grassy Pond is chock-full of flowering Oriental lotus, harrumphing bullfrogs, and iridescent blue dragonflies. There are lovely water views as you walk along the south side of the pond. At the first intersection beyond the pond, take the middle trail straight back up to the visitors center.

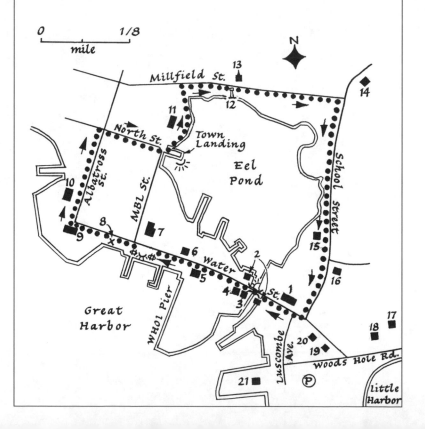

KEY

1. WHOI Redfield Auditorium
2. Restaurants
3. Community Hall
4. Old Firehouse
5. Bigelow Laboratory
6. Candle House
7. MBL Lillie Laboratory
8. Baird Plaque
9. National Marine Fisheries Service
10. Fisheries Aquarium
11. Swope Conference Center
12. Bell Tower
13. St. Joseph's Church
14. Hatch House
15. Woods Hole School
16. Endeavour House (WHOI Exhibit Center)
17. Bradley House
18. Public Library
19. Bakery
20. Post Office
21. Steamship Authority

0   1/8
mile

N

Millfield St.

North St.

Albatross St.

MBL St.

Town Landing

Eel Pond

School Street

Water St.

WHOI Pier

Great Harbor

Luscombe Ave.

Woods Hole Rd.

Little Harbor

Woods Hole

A walking tour of Woods Hole village, with fine water views and marine attractions

Hiking distance: 1¼ miles
Hiking time: 1¼ hours

The quaint, seaside village of Woods Hole has a history that's inextricably tied to the sea. English explorer Bartholomew Gosnold, who is credited with "discovering" Cape Cod, landed at Woods Hole in 1602. By the end of the 1600s, English colonists had purchased Woods Hole from the Wampanoag Indians and established a harborside settlement. The village's economy was spurred by fishing and, later, shipbuilding and whaling. In the 1860s, following the decline in whaling, the Pacific Guano Company became the village's main employer, manufacturing fertilizer from phosphate-rich bird droppings imported from distant Pacific islands.

By the end of the 19th century, Woods Hole was discovered again, this time by marine scientists. Today, it has a number of world-renowned research facilities, including those of the Woods Hole Oceanographic Institution (WHOI) and the Marine Biological Laboratory (MBL). Although the research buildings in Woods Hole are generally not open to the public, the WHOI exhibit center and the National Marine Fisheries Aquarium, both included in this walk, welcome visitors. The MBL offers limited tours by appointment only; call 508-548-3705 for information.

Woods Hole is also the main jumping-off point for ferries to Martha's Vineyard. In summer, there's more bustle in the streets, which, despite the added traffic, adds to the town's unique cosmopolitan appeal. Spring and fall offer an uncrowded scene and a slower pace.

Access

Woods Hole is at the southwest tip of Cape Cod. From Route 28 in Falmouth town center, turn south on Locust Street (which later changes its name to Woods Hole Road), the main road into Woods Hole, 4 miles away.

There's metered parking along Water Street and a pay parking lot at the Steamship Authority ferry terminal. Cyclists will find bike racks at the aquarium.

Trail

This loop walk circles the harborlike Eel Pond, taking in the central streets of the village. Start at the corner of Luscombe Avenue and Water Street, just up from the ferry dock, and begin walking west along Water Street, the village's main street.

You'll almost immediately come to a drawbridge, a good place to linger for a moment and take in the scenic view of Eel Pond. The pond provides a moorage for fishing boats, yachts, and small research vessels. The town still pays homage to seafarers—the drawbridge lifts up and divides the road in two whenever boats need to pass between Eel Pond and Great Harbor.

This end of Water Street sports a couple of good waterfront restaurants and a few interesting shops before giving way to the campuses and offices of the marine research centers.

As you walk over the bridge, you'll pass the community hall, which hosts folk music concerts, square dancing, and other community gatherings, much as it's done since it was built in 1879. The old firehouse next door, retired in 1977, is now used by a food co-op.

The four-story brick building up ahead is the Bigelow Laboratory, which opened in 1931 as the first research center for the Woods Hole Oceanographic Institution (WHOI). It is named for WHOI's first director, biologist Henry Bigelow, and was built with a grant from the Rockefeller Foundation. WHOI, which now gets about 75 percent of its funding from federal grants and contracts, has since grown into the largest independent oceanographic institution in the country.

Candle House, the granite building across the street with the

The picturesque Woods Hole community borders Eel Pond.

ship's bow mounted on its front, gives testimony to an earlier period of Woods Hole's history. It was built in 1836 as a storehouse for out-fitting whalers and was used for manufacturing spermaceti candles until the end of the whaling era. It is now the administrative office for the Marine Biological Laboratory (MBL). Established in 1888, MBL is the oldest marine laboratory in the United States. Among those who have studied at this educational and research center are about 35 Nobel laureates, many of whom received their Nobel recognition for research conducted at the MBL.

A little farther down Water Street is a small park overlooking Great Harbor, with a couple of benches, a sundial, and a good view of the offshore Elizabeth Islands. There's a fair chance you'll find WHOI's 279-foot *Knorr* or one of its other research vessels docked alongside the pier to the left. The low, red brick structure on the west side of the park is a pumping station that draws in seawater for the MBL laboratories.

As you continue down Water Street, you'll pass a plaque dedicated to Spencer Baird, who is credited with establishing Woods Hole as a center for marine studies. Baird convinced Congress to establish the U.S. Commission of Fish and Fisheries (now the National Marine Fisheries Service), and in 1871 he became its first commissioner. He proceeded to build the commission's first laboratory in Woods Hole, which stands as the oldest fisheries laboratory in the world. The National Marine Fisheries Service administrative office is the next building on the left.

Just around the corner, on Albatross Street, is the Fisheries Aquarium. Numerous fish tanks and exhibits are displayed inside, and each summer a couple of harbor seals cavort in a tank out front. The aquarium is open from 10 AM to 4 PM daily in summer, weekdays during the off-season. Admission is free.

Continue walking up Albatross until you reach North Street, then turn right and walk out to the town landing for another good view of Eel Pond. From the landing, walk north along the water side of MBL's Swope Conference Center to Millfield Street. The MBL cafeteria on the ground floor of the Swope building is open to the public weekdays.

Turn right upon reaching Millfield Street, and you'll shortly come to the Angelus bell tower, built of pink granite in 1929. In this science-oriented town, it's perhaps not surprising that one of the two bells is named Mendel—for the 19th-century Austrian monk and botanist—and the other Pasteur, for the French bacteriologist. The bells ring daily at 7 AM, noon, and 6 PM. Inside the gate is a small garden made up entirely of herbs and flowers with biblical names, such as Madonna lily, Saint George's herb, and Our Lady's mantle. Across the street is Saint Joseph's Church (circa 1882), one of the first Catholic churches built on Cape Cod.

Continue down Millfield Street, a quiet, residential street of older, waterside houses, until you reach School Street. Here, if you look up the hill to the left, you'll see Hatch House, a cedar-shingled house built around 1700, one of the oldest homes in the village.

Turn right on School Street and walk along the east side of Eel Pond. After a few minutes, you'll pass Woods Hole School—the gray Victorian building on the knoll overlooking the pond. Listed on the

National Register of Historic Buildings, it was built in 1870 and is one of New England's oldest wooden schoolhouses.

A little farther down on the left is Endeavour House, a former Methodist church that's been converted into WHOI's exhibit center. Inside are videos and displays on WHOI projects. Much of the presentation is dedicated to the deepwater mini-sub *Alvin,* which in 1986 carried scientists to the deck of the sunken *Titanic* and a year later charted Loihi, a new volcanic island building up on the ocean floor off Hawaii. The center, incidentally, is named after the ship of Pacific explorer Captain James Cook, who in 1778 became the first Westerner to discover Hawaii. The center is open daily in summer and on weekends in spring and fall. Admission is free.

Continue down School Street back to Water Street and the start of the loop walk.

If you want to explore further, a few minutes' walk east on Water Street will bring you to the public library and the adjacent Bradley House. This former sea captain's home is now a museum with displays on Woods Hole history, though it's open only in summer. From the museum grounds, there's a view of picturesque Little Harbor, the home of Woods Hole's Coast Guard station.

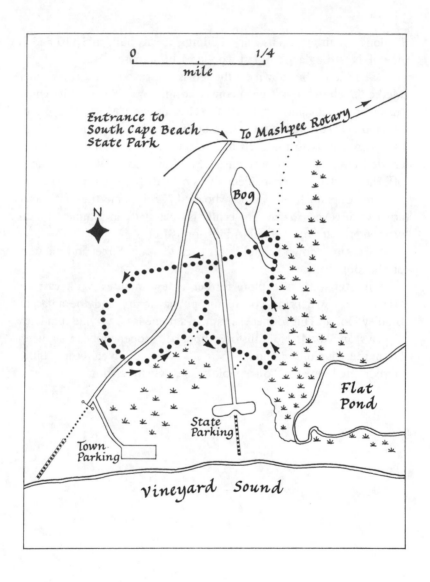

Great Flat Pond Trail

A state park trail encompassing woodlands, marshes, and bogs

Hiking distance: 1½ miles
Hiking time: 1 hour

Great Flat Pond Trail is in South Cape Beach State Park, in the town of Mashpee. The 435-acre park includes a popular ocean beach and borders Waquoit Bay, an estuary that supports a rich variety of marine and animal life. The boundaries of South Cape Beach State Park are within the Waquoit Bay National Estuarine Research Reserve, which was established in 1984 to study estuarine ecology. In addition to ongoing research, the reserve sponsors natural history programs and conducts interpretive walks. Great Flat Pond Trail is officially closed Monday through Saturday during the fall and winter hunting season. For more information, call 508-457-0495.

Shaped somewhat like a butterfly, the Great Flat Pond Trail consists of two wings, each about ¾ mile in length, that connect to form a loop trail. The trail crosses pine-oak woodlands and bogs, with some fine marsh views along the way. The path is in a natural condition, spanned in its wettest parts by simple boardwalks, and it can be a bit muddy, especially after heavy rains.

The trail has a fine variety of wetland and woodland plants. Near the bogs, you'll find sweet pepperbush, blueberry, maleberry, and swamp azalea, the last with clusters of fragrant white flowers in early summer. Wildflowers that grow in the bogs include meadow beauty, a flashy pink flower with inch-wide blossoms and long yellow stamens that blooms all summer, and the insectivorous sundew, whose leaves are covered with sticky, red-tipped hairs. The drier areas between the marsh and the pine-oak forest abound with inkberry and huckleberry. A fair amount of poison ivy edges into the path along

Another gorgeous sunset over the marshland at South Cape Beach State Park

the wooded sections of this walk, so long pants are recommended.

Access

From the Mashpee Rotary in Mashpee, where Routes 28 and 151 merge, take Great Neck Road south 2.7 miles and continue on Great Oak Road another 2 miles. Turn left at the sign for South Cape Beach State Park.

There are two parking areas open to the general public without fees during the off-season. The main road leads into the beachside parking lot run by the town of Mashpee; from 9 AM to 4 PM during the summer beach season, a Mashpee beach parking sticker is required.

Alternatively, a state-run lot is reached by turning left 0.2 mile after the park entrance sign. In the summer, a parking fee of $2 is collected.

We start the trail from the town lot, but as it's a loop trail, it can readily be accessed from either lot.

Trail

The trailhead is at the side of the main road and begins in an area dominated by inkberry shrubs. A member of the holly family, inkberry thrives in moist woods and grows thickly in many places along the trail. This native shrub has smooth, elliptic, evergreen leaves and in the fall produces black berries that attract songbirds.

Just a minute from the trailhead, the path leads to the edge of an open salt marsh. This is one of the prettiest parts of the trail and a good spot for sighting herons and marsh hawks. As it's typically one of the wettest parts of the trail, it's also a good place to gauge whether conditions are going to be muddy along the rest of the walk.

The trail skirts the marsh for a couple of minutes, then comes to a sign that reads EITHER WAY. Turn right, and almost immediately you'll pass a short but overgrown spur trail that leads back to the marsh, providing another good vantage point for birders. The main trail continues on through an area thick with sheep laurel, a heath that blooms with pink flowers from May through July. Sheep laurel is also known as lambkill, because its foliage can be toxic to livestock.

The trail then enters a woods of tall pitch pines, crosses the paved road that leads to the state-run parking lot, and continues on the other side, where it's marked by a triangular blue blaze.

The floor of the pine forest is carpeted with needles and has an abundance of wintergreen, a low-growing evergreen with shiny leaves and bright red berries. Wintergreen leaves were traditionally used to make an aromatic tea, which has earned the plant the nickname teaberry.

The trail winds through the woods and comes into contact with a freshwater marsh, thick with cattails and fed by Flat Pond. At the marsh edge, the trail narrows and continues along an embankment lined with highbush blueberries and swamp azalea. Breaks in the foliage offer some nice glimpses into the marsh, which is often alive with birdsong. Be sure to take a few moments to scan for great blue herons roosting in the nearby pines—we commonly spot one here. Look, too, for pine warblers, a small brown and yellow bird that nests in the trees at the marsh edge.

After leaving the marsh, the trail comes to a fork. Rather than taking the path straight ahead, turn left and take the trail through the woods. Two minutes along, you'll cross a boardwalk over a bog. Shortly beyond that, the trail will again cross the main road. Here you have two choices: You can go straight ahead on the newest addition to the trail network, which loops through mixed woodland, or you can cut your walk short by taking the path that jogs slightly left and leads back to the EITHER WAY sign.

A pleasant beach stroll can be added on to the outing once you get back to the parking area. If you used the town parking lot, you'll be right on the beach. If you used the state parking lot, a boardwalk takes you across the dunes to the shoreline. For the best strolling, head in a westerly direction along the beach—you can either come back the same way or return over the dunes via a second boardwalk about 5 minutes west of the town parking lot.

Yarmouth Nature Trail

A peaceful trail through woodlands and around a small pond

Hiking distance: 1½ miles
Hiking time: 1¼ hours

The Historical Society of Old Yarmouth maintains a fine nature trail in Yarmouthport that passes through varied woodlands, beside wetlands, and around a kettle pond.

The land was settled in 1639 by Anthony Thacher, one of the three original founders of Yarmouth. Thacher cleared the land and established a homestead, grazing cattle and sheep and planting orchards of apple and pear trees. He was so fond of his orchards that his last request was to be buried beneath the pear trees in a site whose location has since been forgotten. The 53-acre property that the hike crosses was gifted to the historical society in 1956 by one of Thacher's descendants.

There are two interconnecting loop trails: the mile-long Main Trail, with interpretive markers, and the ½-mile Pond Trail that curves around the south side of Miller Pond. Although parts of the trail are a little hilly, the walk is easy and pleasant in any season.

Before or after the walk, you might want to take a look at the Captain Bangs Hallet House, just up the slope from the trailhead. The house, whose back side dates to 1740 and whose front and main sections are latter-day Greek Revival, was the home of a prominent Yarmouth sea captain who made his fortune in the China-India trade. Today, the house is the headquarters of the Historical Society of Old Yarmouth and is authentically furnished in typical 19th-century style. Equally impressive is the magnificent, two-hundred-year-old weeping beech tree that dominates the backyard. The interior of the home is open on Thursday and Sunday afternoons in summer; for more details, call the society at 508-362-3021.

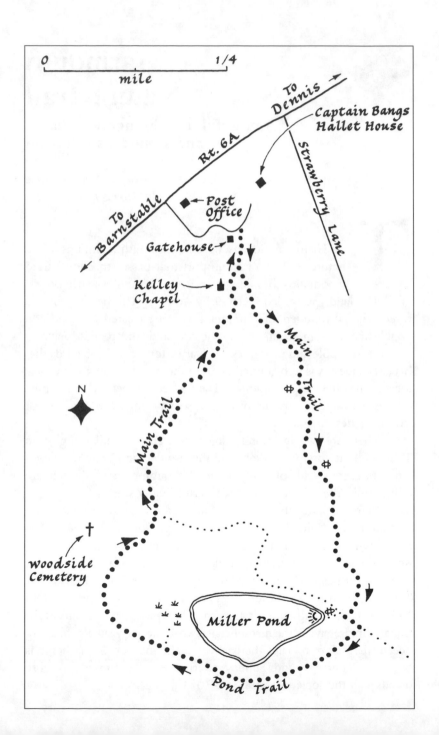

Access

The trail begins behind the Yarmouthport post office on Route 6A in Yarmouthport, 0.9 mile east of the Barnstable/Yarmouth town line and 2.9 miles west of the Dennis/Yarmouth town line. Take the driveway immediately west of the post office and park a few hundred yards down it, opposite the small shingled building known as the gatehouse.

Trail

The trail starts at the left side of the historical society's gatehouse and herb garden. A donation of 50 cents for adults and 25 cents for children is requested; drop the money through the gatehouse door. Here you'll usually find a trail map that identifies trees and other points of interest, which correspond to numbered stone markers along the trail.

The well-worn dirt paths are easy to follow. About 50 yards from the trailhead, the trail forks. Take the path to the left, which is marked by a black arrow painted on stone.

A short way along, a marker on the left identifies an English oak tree, which is distinguishable by its small leaves with short stems and rounded lobes. The trail then goes up through eastern red cedar trees and bayberry bushes to marker #3, which identifies a former pasture where pines, cedars, oaks, and low shrubs are in the process of reclaiming the field.

A few minutes farther, you'll find a bench offering a shady respite beneath a grove of pine trees. The trail continues uphill through an area with rhododendrons that set this neck of the woods abloom in May. A trailside bench sits next to one of the largest rhododendrons.

The trail then passes a newly established oak woods before going down some wooden steps to Miller Pond. We will be following the Pond Trail, which starts off to the left at the fork; but first, make a little detour by turning right and then immediately left down a very short path to the edge of Miller Pond. Here, a bench shaded by a red maple tree provides a scenic view of this woodland pond. Although the shallow waters are devoid of fish, the pond abounds with frogs, and if you arrive near dusk or dawn, you might even spot deer watering along the shore. The surrounding woods also harbors raccoons, rabbits, skunks, squirrels, and quail.

When you're ready to leave the pond, walk back out to the trail and turn right. Continue past the Main Trail you first came down, and, about a minute ahead on the right, you'll see the signposted start of the Pond Trail.

Follow the Pond Trail in a clockwise direction around Miller Pond. This section is a pretty, wooded walk through red and white oaks, pitch pines, and white pines, much of it over a comfortable cushion of pine needles. The tracks from the old Cape railroad are on the left, and there are views of Miller Pond off to the right.

After about 10 minutes, look for an earthen trench on the right, for, just beyond that, a very short spur trail leads down to wetlands where wildflowers and feathery grasses grow. Although you can walk to the edge of the wetlands, the marsh ecology is very fragile, and walking into the marsh is prohibited.

The Pond Trail then goes through a section of tall, thin, thorny locust trees and cherry trees, skirts the edge of the Woodside Cemetery, and climbs through more oaks and pines to meet up with the Main Trail. Go straight ahead on the Main Trail, heading north back toward the trailhead. In addition to the ever-present oaks and pines, the trail passes bushes of Scotch broom and bayberry and low-lying heathers, mosses, pipsissewa, and bearberry, the last taking over the edge of a long-abandoned golf course. Ahead on the right, a white birch tree stands in an open area, one of the few remaining birches that have not yet been choked out by the process of plant succession.

Shortly before the trail merges and returns to the gatehouse, you'll pass another marked English oak on the right, followed by an attractive, lone blue spruce and, a little farther down on the left, the drooping branches of a Norway spruce. Next on the trail is the Kelley Chapel, built in 1873. Like a scene locked in time a hundred years ago, the small chapel still contains whitewashed pews, an old piano, a woodstove, and a pulpit. From here, it's just a few minutes back to the gatehouse.

Indian Lands Conservation Area

A walk through woods and along marsh at the edge of the Bass River

Hiking distance: 2 miles
Hiking time: 1½ hours

Indian Lands Conservation Area, along the banks of the upper Bass River, was the site of a winter encampment for the Nobscusset Indians, who hunted and fished in the river's inlets and marshland. It was the last place in the town of Dennis where Indians were allowed to live following encroachment on their lands by white settlers.

In 1750, the few Indians still at this site were moved to a reservation in what is now the town of Yarmouth, and by the end of the 1700s, the last of the Nobscusset tribe had succumbed to smallpox. A recent archaeological dig in the Indian Lands Conservation Area has uncovered six layers of Indian settlements marked by cooking implements, arrowheads, and piles of discarded shells.

The 6-mile-long Bass River is the largest tidal river on the eastern seaboard. The river is a mix of fresh and salt waters that ebb and flow with the ocean tides and provide good fishing grounds for flounder and striped bass. Nordic explorers led by Leif Ericson are thought to have sailed up the Bass River around 1000 AD. Nowadays the river forms a natural dividing line between the towns of Dennis and Yarmouth.

The trails in Indian Lands skirt a scenic stretch of the river and a beautiful area of unspoiled marshland, where great blue heron are not uncommon.

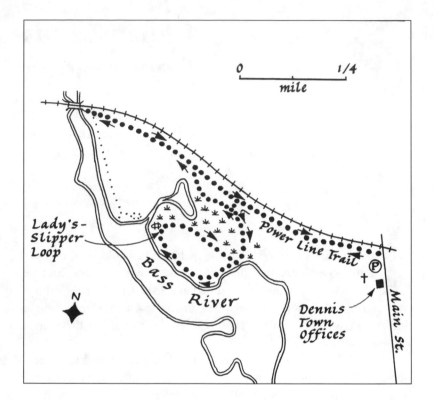

Access

Indian Lands Conservation Area is in the town of Dennis. From Route 6, take exit 9 and drive 0.7 mile south on Route 134 to the third traffic light, there turning right onto Upper County Road. Take the next right turn onto Main Street. After just 0.2 mile, you'll come to the Dennis Town Offices. Park in the north parking lot.

Trail

From the parking lot, look for the power lines north of the cemetery and head down the dirt road that runs alongside them. As you walk, notice the railroad tracks paralleling the trail. They are relics of a bygone era when twice-daily train traffic brought vacationers from New York to the South Dennis station. In less than 10 minutes, the trailhead sign to Indian Lands will be clearly visible on the left. Turn here to start the trail.

Almost immediately after the trailhead, the trail splits. Take the path to the left. In a few minutes you'll come to a clearing with a spectacular view of the marsh on the right and the Bass River on the left. Spanning the river to the south is the High Bank Bridge. In its earliest days, this was a toll bridge between the towns of Dennis and Yarmouth, complete with a tollhouse.

The trail soon divides to make an easy ½-mile circle, sometimes called the Lady's Slipper Loop for the native orchids that bloom along the trail in May. The left side of the loop trail runs along the river, and the right side goes along the tidal marsh and a pretty, pond-shaped inlet. We take the loop in a clockwise direction, though you could just as easily start on the marsh side.

The trees along the river are predominantly pitch pine, and the trail is cushioned with pine needles. There are also oaks, wild pink roses, bayberries, and blueberries, as well as young white pine trees planted by the Dennis Conservation Commission. White pine is a shapely tree with long, feathery needles grouped in fives, differentiated from the more spunky-looking pitch pine, with its spiky, three-needle tufts.

Although there's no development whatsoever along the trail itself, you can look across to houses on the Yarmouth side of the river in what is known as the Blue Rock area. Many of the riverfront homes have their own backyard docks with boats tied up alongside.

Midway along the loop, there's a small bench where you can sit and take in the view. The trail then curves around to the sheltered inlet and tidal marsh, a favorite spot for geese and mallard ducks. It's easy to imagine the Indians of yesteryear quietly slipping their canoes through this pristine area.

Keep an eye out for great blue herons feeding in the marsh. Although they blend in well with the soft green marsh grasses, they're much taller. The largest of the herons, great blues stand 4–5 feet tall and have a 6-foot wingspan.

After completing the loop, follow the trail back out the same way you came. When you reach the fork, just before the trailhead,

These native orchids bloom in abundance along the Lady's Slipper Loop.

turn down the trail to the left, which offers still more marsh views. Within a few minutes you'll come back out at the dirt trail that runs along the power lines.

Continue down the power-line trail to the left. After about 10 minutes, the trail goes up a small hill and ends at the Bass River, which is spanned at this point by a short railroad bridge. From the bridge you can peer up and down the river and get a glimpse of Kellys Bay on the north side of the nearby highway.

If you want to explore further, take the 15-minute side trail that leads off to the right as you start to head back down the hill. Not far from the start of this trail, large clumps of lilacs mark a former home-site, which is now overrun with poison ivy. The side trail runs south above the river through a woods of pitch pine and scrub oak and ends at the opposite side of the same marsh inlet you saw earlier from the Lady's Slipper Loop. Return the same way you walked in or take one of the smaller and more overgrown paths to get back to the power-line trail.

Follow the power-line trail straight back to the parking lot.

11

John Wing Trail

A trail to an upland
island surrounded by a
salt marsh and on to an
undeveloped beach on
Cape Cod Bay

Hiking distance: 1½ miles
Hiking time: 1 hour

The John Wing Trail combines several short, interconnecting paths on 140 acres of conservation land owned by the town of Brewster. The walk leads across a salt marsh to upland woods and then out to the beach, offering scenic coastal and marshland views. This easy hike has good birding, for the marsh provides habitat for numerous birds, including great blue herons, green herons, American kestrels, and red-winged blackbirds.

Most of the walk is on Wing Island, a raised, wooded island surrounded by salt marsh. The trail is named for John Wing, the first European settler in the area, who built a house on the island in 1656. The isolated setting offered Wing and his family a peaceful retreat from the religious persecution they had suffered as Quakers in the staunchly Puritan town of Sandwich.

Although you can now walk across the marsh to the island, in John Wing's day the island was surrounded by water and access was by rowboat. Even these days, the marsh surrounding the island is often flooded during high tide, so it's best to time your walk to coincide with low tide. The Cape Cod Museum of Natural History keeps a tide clock (call 508-896-3867), and there's also a daily tide chart in the *Cape Cod Times* (see "Wellfleet, Bay Side"). If you miss low tide, you may prefer to walk the museum's North and South Trails (hike 12).

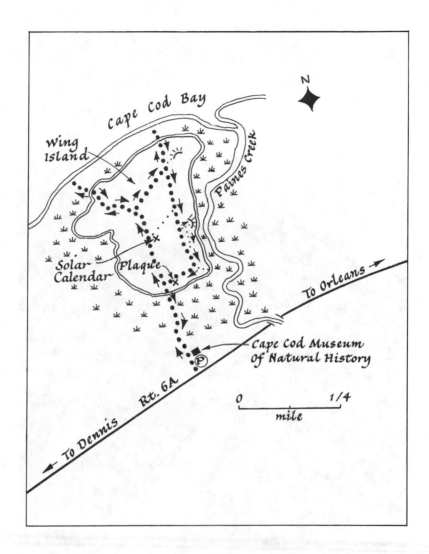

An interpretive brochure that discusses the flora and fauna along the trails can be picked up at the museum for a nominal fee.

Access

The John Wing Trail starts at the Cape Cod Museum of Natural History, which is on the north side of Route 6A in Brewster, 1.6

A boardwalk across the marsh provides access to Wing Island.

miles east of the Dennis/Brewster town line and 6.3 miles west of the Orleans/Brewster town line.

Trail

The trail begins in a pine woods at the left side of the museum. From there, it's just a couple of minutes down to the marsh, where the trail passes through head-high salt reed grass and a variety of lower grasses, rushes, and sedges. The section across the muddy marsh, which once had to be crossed with only the benefit of a blanket of marsh hay, is now spanned by a boardwalk that should keep your feet dry at all but the highest tides.

After crossing the marsh, take the spur trail to the right for about 50 feet to reach a plaque marking the site where John Wing built his house. Then return to the original trail and continue straight ahead through a wooded area of eastern red cedar, oak, and pine trees. Interpretive post #5 marks an overgrown field where wildflowers bloom in season. One of the most spectacular is the New England blazing star, whose stalk stands 3 feet tall and is ablaze with dozens of bushy, pink-purple flower heads in August and September. The field is also the site of a stone solar calendar recently installed by Cape resident Jeff Thibodeau. The circle of stones marks the four cardinal points as well as sunset and sunrise at the solstice.

As the trail continues past the field, you'll come successively to two forks. Bear left at both of them, following the trail through the woods, off the island, out across the marsh, and down to the beach. At low tide, you can walk far out across the exposed tidal flats and onto emerging sandbars that reach like fingers out into the bay.

When you're ready to continue, walk back up to Wing Island from the beach on the same trail you came down. In late summer, sea lavender flowers add a pale purple mist to the salt meadow hay in the marsh that separates the island from the beach. The marsh is also a good vantage point for looking up at Wing Island and observing how it truly is a distinct, upland island rising above the coastal flats.

About 5 minutes back up the trail from the beach, you'll come to a fork. Take the trail to the left through a wooded area, until it leads into another trail. Bear left, and almost immediately you'll come to a fork just above the marsh. The short path to the right leads to an over-look with a pretty view of Cape Cod Bay.

After enjoying the view, continue along the trail, across the marsh, over the dunes, and down to the beach. There are beach plum bushes along this part of the trail that are loaded with white flowers in May and that bear small fruit that ripen in late summer. Beach plum jelly made from these fruits is a specialty of Cape Cod.

When you're finished exploring the beach, come back up the trail and continue straight ahead, bearing left at the fork where you entered this trail as well as at the next fork. At the third fork, a short walk to the left leads to a fine view of open marsh cut by the me-andering Paines Creek.

Continue south on the main trail, then bear right at the next fork for a short walk back to John Wing's homestead site and the return walk across the marsh to the museum.

North and South Trails

Two short walks through marsh and woodlands

Hiking distance: 1 mile
Hiking time: 1 hour

The Cape Cod Museum of Natural History in Brewster is the starting point for the ¼-mile North Trail and the ¾-mile South Trail. Both trails are on lands owned by the museum, cross woodlands and marsh, and are easy walking, although the North Trail can be a bit wet, especially at high tide.

The Cape Cod Museum of Natural History has exhibits of the flora and fauna found in Cape Cod's varied natural environments. Some of the highlights include an excellent display of many of the birds common to the Cape, live fish and turtle tanks, and a good seashell collection.

The museum is open year-round 9:30 AM–4:30 PM Monday through Saturday and 11–4:30 on Sundays. Admission is $5 for adults, $2 for children ages 5–12, and free for children under 5. The museum sponsors numerous natural history programs year-round, including field walks, owl prowls, wildlife programs, lectures, and films. For more information, call 508-896-3867.

Access

The Cape Cod Museum of Natural History is on Route 6A in Brewster, 1.6 miles east of the Dennis/Brewster town line and 6.3 miles west of the Orleans/Brewster town line. The museum and the North Trail are on the north side of Route 6A, the South Trail is on the south side, and there are parking lots at both. Use caution when crossing Route 6A, because the traffic moves quickly.

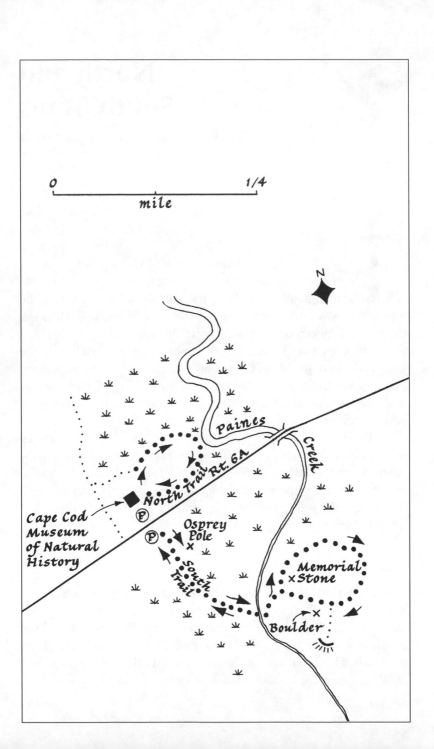

North Trail

The North Trail starts at the back side of the Cape Cod Museum of Natural History. The best approach is to begin with a visit to the museum, where displays provide an in-depth look at Cape Cod ecology. On the lower level, after the last exhibit, exit through the back door, where a short path leads left to the trailhead.

The ¼-mile trail begins in a transition zone where the wooded upland meets the salt marsh. It then quickly enters the high-marsh zone, a brackish environment at the very edge of the marsh that is generally flooded only during storm tides. Only those plants that can tolerate some salinity, such as seaside goldenrod and freshwater cordgrass, are able to grow here.

The trail then continues into the salt marsh itself, passing over spongy peat and offering fine marsh views. In places, the path is covered with salt hay, which helps keep your feet dry. This part of the marsh, called a salt meadow, is thick with salt grasses that were once cut and harvested by farmers as fodder for their sheep and cattle. The wooded mound you see to the north is Wing Island, an upland island completely surrounded by marsh. (The John Wing Trail, which goes out to Wing Island, is hike 11.)

As you continue walking straight ahead, you'll come to the edge of Paines Creek, which cuts across the marsh before emptying into Cape Cod Bay. The trail then loops back to the museum, curving up out of the salt marsh and into the low uplands where arrowwood, highbush blueberry, and shadbush grow. A quick walk through the woods then leads back to the edge of the museum, where there's a small garden of woodland wildflowers.

South Trail

The ¾-mile South Trail begins at the museum's overflow parking lot, on the south side of Route 6A. The trail leads down from the east side of the parking lot and passes through a mixed woods before coming to the edge of a marsh. One of the more common shrubs near the marsh edge is arrowwood, a member of the viburnum family. Arrowwood can be identified by its teardrop-shaped leaves with sharply serrated edges and by its straight, smooth shoots that were once used by American Indians to make arrow shafts.

The trail then leads out over a brackish cattail marsh, crossing several small footbridges over ditches used for mosquito control. These ditches not only drain the marsh of the stagnant surface water that provides ideal mosquito breeding grounds but also bring in thousands of minnows with incoming tides to feed on the mosquito eggs laid in the marsh. Outgoing tides then flush out the ditches, carrying more of the mosquito eggs and larvae away.

After crossing the first footbridge, you'll notice a weathered trailside osprey pole that attracted its first pair of nesting osprey in 1998.

The last footbridge crosses Paines Creek, which is thick with schools of alewives (called herring on Cape Cod) in late April and May. The fish live most of their lives in the open ocean but return each spring to spawn in the waters of the freshwater stream or pond where they were hatched. Herring gulls feast at Paines Creek when the herring are running, and it's a good time to sight kingfishers as well.

After crossing Paines Creek, the trail leaves the marsh and enters a beech forest. Follow the main trail to the left as it continues above the edge of the marsh. About 100 yards down, you'll find a stone with a memorial plaque dedicated to Robert Taft Olmstead, in whose memory part of this land was contributed to the museum. You've now started to make a loop. Follow the trail past the plaque, and the path will shortly come to an old split-rail fence and curve up to the right. As you go uphill, the beech trees begin to give way to oaks and tall pitch pines. The area on the east side of the loop was once a cranberry bog, but it's now almost completely overgrown with catbrier and scrub and there's little left to see.

Just before the trail goes back down the hill to complete the loop, a side trail heads off to the left, marked by a large boulder. A two-minute excursion on this trail will bring you to a scenic overview of the marsh and Paines Creek. This side trail once continued all the way down to Stony Brook Grist Mill, a popular spot for watching the herring run. All that remains now, however, is a deer trail.

After completing the loop, retrace your steps back across the marsh to the parking lot.

A nesting osprey surveys the marsh along the South Trail.

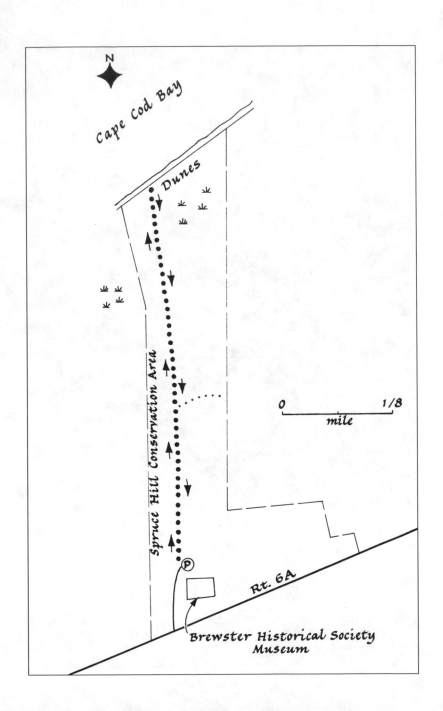

Spruce Hill Trail

A nice, short walk through woods to scenic Cape Cod Bay

Hiking distance: 1 mile
Hiking time: 30 minutes

The Spruce Hill Conservation Area is a 25-acre property that was purchased by the town of Brewster in 1985. The land, previously known as the Castiglioni estate, is long and narrow, stretching from Route 6A to Cape Cod Bay.

The Spruce Hill Trail, which runs the length of the property, makes for a very pleasant stroll through typical Cape Cod scenery. Adding to its appeal is the fact that the trail is not yet widely known and is only lightly used. The Brewster Conservation Commission maintains the trail.

The home at the front of the property (circa 1840) houses the Brewster Historical Society Museum, which is open during the summer season. The house is surrounded by lofty Norway spruce trees that were planted to provide a windbreak from the blustery winter winds that whip across the bay from the north.

Access

The trail starts behind the Brewster Historical Society Museum, 3341 Route 6A, East Brewster. If you're coming from the west, take Route 6A and turn left at the first driveway after passing Cape Cod Sea Camp Wono, 6 miles east of the Dennis/Brewster town line. If you're approaching from the east, you'll turn right into the museum driveway 0.6 mile past the entrance to Nickerson State Park.

This treat of a view awaits hikers at the end of the short Spruce Hill Trail.

Trail

The trail starts at the left side of the parking lot and heads north, sloping very gradually as it runs straight down to the beach. The wide, grassy path is actually an old carriage road that was used a century ago for transporting goods to and from boats in the bay. Local lore suggests that it was also used for midnight runs by bootleggers during the Prohibition era.

The beginning of the trail is in a thickly wooded area dominated by pitch pines and various oaks. Typical woodland wildflowers, such as pink lady's slippers and starflowers, bloom here in spring.

As it gets closer to the sea, the trail brushes a couple of marshy areas where tupelo trees grow. Tupelo, or black gum, has distinctive horizontal branches that come out of the trunk at right angles. Its smooth, oval leaves turn a fiery red in autumn. As you approach the low dunes near the sea, the vegetation gives way to eastern red cedar and low bushy beach plums, the latter thick with white blossoms from late May to early June.

On the edge of the dunes above the beach, there's a lovely coastal view of waving beach grass, white sands, and the curving coastline of the lower Cape. On a clear day you can see Provincetown's Long Point and Wood End lighthouses straight ahead across the bay.

If you feel like lingering, the beach makes a fine place for a short stroll or picnic. To return, head straight back on the same trail.

14

Cliff Pond Trail

A walk around the perimeter of a large freshwater pond

Hiking distance: 3¼ miles
Hiking time: 2 hours

The Cliff Pond Trail is an easy walk that circles the largest pond in Nickerson State Park. In summer, the park is heavily used and can be a bit noisy; but in the off-season, Nickerson is mostly visited by fishermen, cyclists, and hikers and is a quiet and peaceful place to walk.

Nickerson, the fourth largest state park in Massachusetts, came into the public domain in 1934 when Addie Nickerson donated 1,700 acres of her estate in memory of her son, Roland C. Nickerson Jr., who had died in a flu epidemic. The following year, the Civilian Conservation Corps began building roads, clearing campsites, and planting thousands of white pines and other trees.

Today, Nickerson State Park is a popular recreation area, with more than four hundred campsites and good pond swimming, boating, trout fishing, and hiking. The route around the 193-acre Cliff Pond, one of Nickerson's eight ponds, is the longest hiking trail in the park. All of the ponds are kettle ponds, created by depressions from huge blocks of ice left behind by retreating glaciers about fifteen thousand years ago. As you walk around Cliff Pond, you'll come across a couple of shoreline glacial erratics—large boulders carried down from the mainland by those same glaciers.

Because Nickerson is both inland and wooded, the park attracts woodpeckers, blue jays, nuthatches, larks, thrushes, wrens, ruffed grouse, great horned owls, and screech owls. Its ponds draw

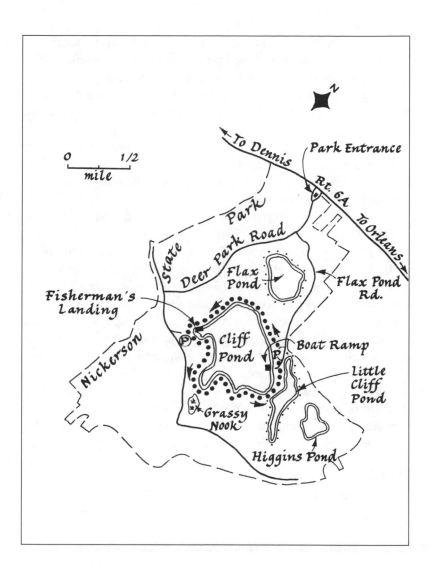

N

To Dennis

Park Entrance

Rt. 6A

To Orleans

State Park

Deer Park Road

Flax Pond

Flax Pond Rd.

Fisherman's Landing

Nickerson

Cliff Pond

Boat Ramp

P

Little Cliff Pond

Grassy Nook

Higgins Pond

0   1/2
mile

numerous waterfowl, including common and hooded mergansers, common goldeneyes, pied-billed grebes, and ring-necked ducks. The bald eagle, reintroduced to Massachusetts just a decade ago, has made appearances at Nickerson in recent years. Four-legged creatures residing in the park include raccoons, skunks, white-tailed deer, and red fox.

In addition to the Cliff Pond Trail described here, the park maintains shorter hiking trails around Little Cliff Pond and Flax Pond and 8 miles of paved, off-road bicycle trails through the woods that make for good strolling.

Access

The entrance to Nickerson State Park is clearly marked on Route 6A in Brewster, 6.8 miles east of the Dennis/Brewster town line and 1.1 miles west of the Orleans/Brewster town line. After passing through the park gate, continue 0.4 mile and then turn left onto Flax Pond Road, the first road beyond the entrance. The sign at the turn is marked AREA 5 and BOAT RAMP. Follow this road 1.2 miles to its end, where there's a parking lot above the boat ramp.

There are no fees to enter Nickerson State Park, though day visitors must leave by 8 PM. Campsites are available for a small fee, but because of the park's popularity, it can be difficult to get a space. About half of the campsites are on a first-come basis, while the other half can be reserved in advance by calling 508-896-4615.

Trail

The hike closely follows the perimeter of Cliff Pond, alternately skirting the water's edge and climbing through the woods just above the shore. Because the pond is not stream fed but is entirely dependent on groundwater and rainfall, its water level varies from year to year. In periods of little rain, it's possible to walk completely around the pond right at the water's edge.

We take the trail in a counterclockwise direction from the parking lot. The trail is straightforward and clearly blazed the entire length with blue markers put up by the Appalachian Mountain Club. It begins in a woods of scrub oaks and pines, with a smattering of

Canoers enjoy a sunny day on Cliff Pond.

fragrant wintergreen along the trail's edge. A few minutes along, a section of thickly planted pines shades the trail and provides a soft cushion of pine needles underfoot. After about 15 minutes down the trail, you'll come to an attractive white sand beach, soon followed by a second nice curve of sand backed by pines.

After passing these sandy stretches, the beachfront is largely rocky, until you reach the first of three coves. The first cove, dubbed Fisherman's Landing, has a boat ramp and a small beach. As the name suggests, it's well used by fishermen, and along this section of the trail you'll probably spot a few people fishing in rowboats and canoes.

Just beyond Fisherman's Landing, you'll pass thickets of sweet pepperbush and highbush blueberries. In autumn, their bright yellow and red foliage make this spot one of the most scenic on the trail. Wildflowers, some rare and endangered, also grow in this area along the shoreline. The path to the second cove is a pleasant walk that passes through a mixed woods, which includes maple, tupelo, and white pine trees.

After the trail descends out of the woods at the head of the second cove, it goes over a narrow neck between Cliff Pond and Grassy Nook, a freshwater marsh. This very scenic and serene area offers good birding possibilities.

From here, it's about a 20-minute walk to the third and final cove, a pretty little nook with a white sand beach backed by pine and oak trees. It's then about 20 minutes more back to the parking lot. The final section of the trail passes over the narrow jut of land that separates Cliff Pond from Little Cliff Pond, offering views of both.

Monomoy National Wildlife Refuge

A gem of a hike that combines a lovely beach walk and great birding

Hiking distance: 1½ miles
Hiking time: 1½ hours

Monomoy National Wildlife Refuge, the only national wilderness area in southern New England, is located in Chatham, on the "elbow" of Cape Cod. Although most of the refuge's 2,750 acres consists of two offshore islands accessible only by boat, 40 acres are connected to the mainland by a dike. This part of the refuge, called Morris Island, includes the refuge headquarters, a marked interpretive trail, and a beautiful stretch of beach backed by cliffs, sand dunes, and salt marsh.

Monomoy's story is one of ongoing erosion and shifting sands. Until 1958, all the land in the refuge was part of Monomoy Point, a narrow, 8-mile-long barrier beach stretching southward from Chatham. But that year, tempestuous surf from winter storms broke through the barrier beach, separating the peninsula from the mainland and creating Monomoy Island. Twenty years later, the powerful nor'easter that brought the "Blizzard of '78" to the Boston area hit Monomoy with such force that it divided the island in two.

North Monomoy Island, 2½ miles long, consists of sand dunes with beach grass, tidal flats, and salt marsh. The 5-mile-long South Monomoy Island is more diverse, with woodlands and freshwater ponds in addition to sandy beaches, dunes, and marshland.

Both islands are havens for wildlife, including wintering seals

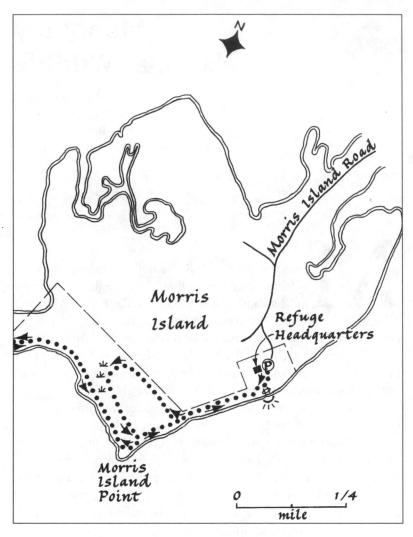

and tens of thousands of sea- and shorebirds, some that just pass through during their annual spring and fall migrations and others that stay the summer to nest. Many people consider South Monomoy, which is also rich with land birds, to be the finest bird-watching site in the Northeast. All in all, nearly 300 species of birds have been identified at the refuge.

The endangered piping plover nests at Monomoy, as do spotted and least sandpipers. The most colorful of the nesting shorebirds is the American oystercatcher. It has a vibrant orange beak shaped like an oyster knife, which it inserts into oysters and other shellfish, slicing through the muscle to open the shell.

The refuge also has a great variety of waterfowl. Winter's cold draws rafts of sea ducks, including up to 100,000 common eiders. In fact, so many eiders are drawn to Monomoy that during the wintertime they're rarely spotted elsewhere in the Northeast. Other birds found at the refuge are black-crowned night herons, northern harriers, snowy egrets, and cormorants, and, although not as common, we've also spotted an American kestrel, a Cooper's hawk, and a red-tailed hawk while hiking at Morris Island.

Although Morris Island, with its human presence and smaller size, is less favored by wildlife than the isolated North and South Monomoy Islands, it is nevertheless an excellent site for bird-watching and has a fine diversity of both land and shorebirds. All the habitats found on South and North Monomoy Islands are also found on Morris Island, including marshland, dunes, tidal flats, and woodlands of scrub oak and pitch pine.

An important note: The beach and trail are closed at high tide. To find out about the tides, call the wildlife refuge at 508-945-0594 or check the *Cape Cod Times.*

Access

Morris Island is 2 miles from Chatham town center. Enter Chatham by heading east on Route 28 from Harwich. Or, from Route 6, get off at exit 11, take Route 137 south to Route 28, and turn left.

In Chatham center, Route 28 becomes Main Street, which you follow to its end, turning right onto Shore Road. Just past the Coast Guard station and lighthouse, there's a tricky fork where you take Morris Island Road straight ahead (rather than taking Bridge Street as it curves to the right). Follow Morris Island Road across the dike. Signs will lead you to the refuge headquarters, where there are nine parking spaces. Pick up an interpretive brochure from the box outside the headquarters.

A herring gull perches on a trailhead sign on North Monomoy Island.

Trail

This hike combines the refuge's ¾-mile interpretive trail, which heads down the beach and then loops through woodlands and marsh before coming back along the shore, with a walk across the sand flats to the south end of Morris Island.

The trail starts at the left side of the refuge headquarters in a tiny meadow, where there are a couple of birdhouses that attract tree swallows. Squawky red-winged blackbirds also nest in the area from spring through fall.

Beyond the field, the trail enters a wooded area, and, immediately to the left, there's an overlook and a bench perched on a cliff above the beach. The large, protected body of water you look across is South Way, a feeding area for many of the refuge's waterbirds. The sandy beach across the water was a contiguous part of Cape Cod National Seashore's Nauset Beach until a huge winter storm in 1987 washed away a midsection of the beach, creating a new island now known as South Beach Island. (To get a better look at this "Chatham break," as the washed-out section is known locally, stop at the Chatham Coast Guard Station after leaving the refuge.) From the overlook, you can also see North Monomoy Island to the far right, with South Monomoy in the distance beyond.

In addition to the numerous birds, the islands are a refuge for a few thousand harbor seals that come down from colder northern waters to winter here. A growing number of harbor seals are becoming year-round residents. Less common are gray seals, although they, too, are making a comeback. In 1989, gray seals gave birth on South Monomoy Island, marking the first time in almost a hundred years that gray seal pups had been born on Cape Cod. From the overlook, you can sometimes spot the seals feeding in the waters of South Way.

The trail then descends a wooden stairway that leads down the bank to the beach. A bird feeder along the way attracts cardinals, chickadees, and other woodland birds.

You'll notice fallen trees along the cliff face and the exposed roots of oak trees on the eroding hill above the beach. Since the recent break in Nauset's barrier beach, tides have been higher and winter storms have swept in with much greater force, resulting in an ongoing erosion of the cliff. Sections of this beach were woodlands just a few years ago, and as you walk along the beach flats at low tide, you might well come across the waterworn remains of a tree stump rooted in the sand and encrusted with barnacles.

About 100 yards down the beach, take the path to the right that leads inland through low dunes. Beach grass shortly gives way to poverty grass, lichen, and low-growing pitch pines. As you continue along the trail, notice how the pine trees gradually grow taller as you get farther away from blustery ocean winds.

The woods is a nesting site for pine warblers and a stop-off point for dozens of other warblers that migrate through in spring and fall. At marker #6, you'll find shadbush, which produces white flowers in early May; bayberry bushes, which develop waxy gray berries over the summer; and a few highbush blueberries, which fruit in August.

After a few minutes, the trail leads to a salt marsh, with waters that rise and fall with the tides. To the right of trail marker #8, juniper trees with their lower greenery nibbled away provide evidence of the white-tailed deer that visit the marsh. On the opposite side of the trail from the marker, wintergreen provides a fragrant ground cover.

From the marsh, the trail leads back out to one of the loveliest sections of the beach, a jut of land called Morris Island Point.

At the shoreline, turn right and walk about ⅓ mile, until you get to the end of the beach. Just how far you'll be able to walk depends on the tides. During low tide, beautifully rippled sandbars emerge, and you can walk far out across the shallows.

The sand flats are rich with shellfish. Vast mussel beds stretch along the shoreline, and you can watch herring gulls feasting on crabs or dropping clams from on high until the shells crack open just wide enough for a bill to poke in. These flats are also popular with shell fishermen, and in season at low tide you can expect to see them digging for soft-shelled clams.

To finish the walk, return along the beach back to the stairway and up to the refuge headquarters.

If this short Morris Island trail has whetted your appetite for further exploration of the Monomoy area, you'll be happy to know that both the Cape Cod Museum of Natural History in Brewster (508-896-3867) and the Wellfleet Bay Wildlife Sanctuary (508-349-2615) run boat tours with naturalist guides for day trips to North and South Monomoy Islands. In addition, the decommissioned lighthouse and keeper's quarters on South Monomoy have been restored and are occasionally used for overnight trips organized by the museum.

Fort Hill

A varied hike that offers some of the finest coastal vistas on Cape Cod

Hiking distance: 2 miles
Hiking time: 1½ hours

The Cape Cod National Seashore's Fort Hill hike skirts above the strikingly scenic Nauset Marsh and winds through a swamp of red maple trees. It also passes remnants from the settlements of both Nauset Indians and latter-day colonists and takes in the home of a 19th-century sea captain.

The expansive Nauset Marsh is thick with grasses that are lush green in summer and golden brown in winter. But the area wasn't always this way. When the French explorer Samuel de Champlain arrived in 1605 to chart this area of New France, he found a large, open bay that his ships were able to navigate. Since that time, however, a barrier beach has developed along the mouth of the bay, slowly transforming Nauset Bay into Nauset Marsh.

The first colonists to settle in Nauset arrived from Plymouth in 1644. In contrast to the Nauset Indians, who had lived in close harmony with their environment, these early settlers immediately began to clear-cut the forest. They planted grain, vegetables, and fruit trees and raised cows and sheep. To protect their grazing animals, bounties were offered for wolves; to protect their crops, birds and small animals were killed. The early settlers started a land alteration pattern that would, by the 1800s, turn the Eastham forests into plains with little topsoil and serious erosion problems. One of the last farms in Eastham was here at Fort Hill, a marginal operation that continued until the 1940s.

The Fort Hill hike consists of two connecting trails: the Fort Hill Trail and the Red Maple Swamp Trail. Although a wonderful

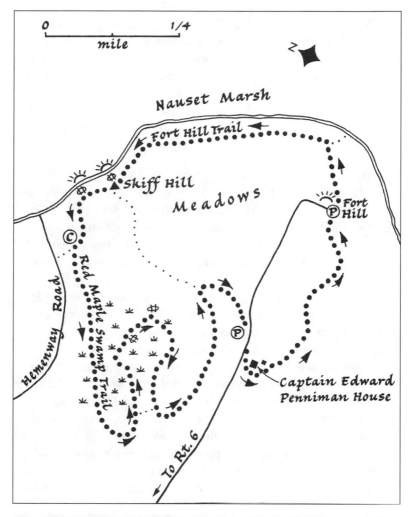

hike for all seasons, Fort Hill is a favorite fall spot for Cape Codders, who come to admire the golden hues of the marsh and to walk through the colorful foliage of the red maple swamp. With its variety of habitats, the Fort Hill area is also considered one of the top birding areas on the Cape.

The hike is of easy to moderate difficulty, with some log-reinforced steps and a couple of moderate slopes.

Access

The turnoff to Fort Hill is clearly marked on Route 6 in Eastham, 1.5 miles north of the rotary that marks the Orleans/Eastham town line and 1.4 miles south of the Salt Pond Visitor Center. The turn is onto Governor Prence Road, which you follow 0.5 mile to its end at the top of Fort Hill. If the top parking lot is full, there's a lower lot across from the Captain Penniman House, where you could also begin the trail.

Trail

From the trailhead at the top of Fort Hill, there's a magnificent view out across Nauset Marsh. The channel at the far right is part of Town Cove, which divides the towns of Eastham and Orleans. Straight out beyond the marsh are the long stretches of barrier beach that buffer Nauset Marsh from the open ocean—Nauset Beach to the right, Coast Guard Beach to the left.

The trail begins along a path of crushed clamshells that leads down the grassy hillside toward the marsh. About 5 minutes down the trail you'll come to a large boulder, the first of a number of glacial erratics deposited around Fort Hill during the Ice Age. A short spur to the right leads down to the marsh and a popular local fishing spot.

The main trail continues to the north, its marsh side skirting a thin strip of low cedars, bayberry, honeysuckle, and wild rose. On the left side of the trail are gently sloping meadows that are divided by long stone walls, a reminder of the days when Fort Hill was a farm. Contrary to the more common policy of allowing nature to take its course, the National Seashore mows these meadows to prevent reforestation—a practice that not only retains the farming-era appearance but also preserves the sweeping views from the hilltop.

After passing the last stone wall, the trail winds through a thicket of red cedar trees on its way to Skiff Hill, where there's a lovely view and an open-air shelter with interpretive plaques on Nauset ecology and history. In front of the shelter is a 20-ton rock that was once used by the Nauset Indians for sharpening stone adzes and shaping bone fishhooks. Run your hands over the rock to feel the smooth surfaces and deep grooves.

If you have binoculars, the lookout provides a good vantage point for spotting the many birds that feed off the marsh, including stately great blue herons, smaller green herons, black-crowned night herons, greater yellowlegs, marsh hawks, and common terns.

When you're ready to leave Skiff Hill, take the paved path that leads west. In about 100 yards, there's a final marsh vista point with a head-on view of the old Coast Guard station. This section of the marsh is a mooring area for small rowboats and is wonderfully picturesque. A couple of benches at the viewpoint invite you to stop and take it all in.

A few minutes beyond the last viewpoint, just past the rest rooms, you'll come to the start of the Red Maple Swamp Trail on the left. The trail immediately leads down to a boardwalk and begins crossing a marshy swamp that harbors large red maple trees. Red maples are red year-round: The shoots and buds are red in winter, the flowers blossom red in spring, the leaf stems are bright red in summer, and the leaves begin to turn reddish in early fall. By mid-October, the Red Maple Swamp Trail is lit with a bright scarlet glow, made all the more delightful by the colorful leaves floating in the water beneath the boardwalk.

Although the trees in the red maple swamp are mature, the woodland is a second-growth forest. Not only did the early settlers down all the original trees, but after depleting their sources of firewood, they then harvested peat from the swamp. Although these vigorous maple trees sent up new growth from their stumps, the effects of the overharvesting remain. The sprout clumps of the felled trees gave rise to multiple trunks, a growth pattern that makes the relatively brittle maple more vulnerable to powerful winds. When Hurricane Bob hit Cape Cod head-on in August 1991, some of these leaning trunks tore off the trees, while other maples were entirely uprooted from the soggy marsh floor.

A little more than 10 minutes after starting down the Red Maple Swamp Trail, you'll reach a junction in the winding path. Go left to make a pleasant, 10-minute loop through the center of the swamp. There are two places with benches along the boardwalk, though in summer the mosquitoes come out in force upon those who

The old Captain Edward Penniman House as seen through its unique whalebone gate

linger too long. Here, as elsewhere along the trail, signs identify some of the flora that you pass. Two delectable specimens along the loop are highbush blueberries and European raspberries.

A few minutes after completing the loop, the trail heads out of the swamp through a thick wood dominated by fragrant cedar trees and bayberry bushes. After climbing up some log-reinforced steps, the trail forks. Go right, and you'll come out on the west side of the meadows. Continue walking to the right for about 5 minutes to reach the lower parking lot.

On the other side of the road is the Captain Edward Penniman House, a decorative sea captain's house built in the Second French Empire style. Penniman made his fortune in the whaling trade, starting his career as a harpooner and ending it as a sea captain. After circling the globe seven times, he returned to his hometown to build this house in 1867. It was an elegant house for its time, with a cupola that provided a clear view of the sea, a huge whalebone gate, and furnishings Penniman had collected on his voyages. Tours of the inside of the house are conducted periodically by the National Seashore; at other times, you'll have to be content with peeking through the windows.

The trail continues at the rear of the house, running in back of the old barn and through a wooded area of black locust trees and wild roses. About 10 minutes from the house, the trail comes out into a clearing just below the Fort Hill parking lot.

Nauset Marsh Trail

A picturesque trail along the edge of Salt Pond and Nauset Marsh

Hiking distance: 1 mile
Hiking time: 45 minutes

Like all salt marshes, Nauset Marsh provides a fragile link between the land and the sea. Incoming tides flood the marsh, sweeping in microscopic organisms and depositing them on the marsh edges. These organisms, coupled with the marsh's abundant plant life, provide food for the many marine creatures that use the shallow, protected salt marsh as a nursery. Indeed, the majority of all shellfish and ocean fish harvested commercially have spent at least part of their lives in the salt-marsh habitat. At low tide, as the water drains out, nutrient-rich mudflats are exposed and tidal pools formed, creating a rich feeding ground for birds. Herons feed on small fish and crabs in the tidal pools, swallows fly above the marsh feasting on mosquitoes, and marsh hawks hunt the upper marsh for small rodents.

The Nauset Marsh Trail is an easy loop walk that skirts the edge of Salt Pond, winds up a hill for a sweeping view of Nauset Marsh, and ends in woodlands. Interpretive markers along the way identify pitch pine, black cherry, eastern red cedar, beach plum, salt-spray rose, and numerous other trailside flora.

The trail begins at the Cape Cod National Seashore's Salt Pond Visitor Center. The center itself is well worth a stop before beginning the hike. It has a small museum with displays depicting the history, geology, and ecology of the Lower Cape, interesting short films that are shown throughout the day, a gift shop with maps and books on

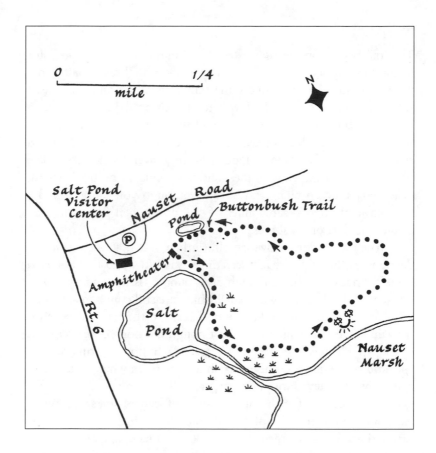

Cape Cod, and rest rooms and drinking water. Salt Pond Visitor Center is open daily year-round, and entrance to the Cape Cod National Seashore is free.

Access

Salt Pond Visitor Center is on Route 6 in Eastham. Turn off Route 6 at the traffic lights by the Cape Cod National Seashore entrance sign, which is 3 miles north of the rotary that marks the Orleans/Eastham town line and 3.1 miles south of the Wellfleet/Eastham town line.

Trail

The trail begins on the right side of the outdoor amphitheater, just below the visitors center. After a short walk, you'll reach Salt Pond, where you turn left and follow the trail along the pond's northeast side. Salt Pond is one of the few kettle ponds on the Lower Cape to have been breached by the ocean, and its water level rises and falls with the tides. Marsh cordgrass and sea lavender grow along the pond side of the trail, the latter abloom with tiny lavender flowers in late summer. The inland side of the pond is dominated by black locust, oaks, cedars, beach plum, and bayberry, though you can also find a few old apple trees—a reminder of the days when Salt Pond had colonial settlers on its shores.

The trail continues over an old earthen dike that once served to dam up a niche of the marsh, creating a shallow pond that attracted game for duck hunters. Although duck hunting is no longer allowed on Nauset Marsh, boating and shellfishing are still common activities.

At the end of the dike, the trail veers to the left and goes inland up some log-reinforced steps through a woods of eastern red cedar. After a few minutes, you'll reach a hilltop clearing with a splendid panorama of Nauset Marsh and benches where you can sit and enjoy the view. From here, the trail climbs up and down a few gentle hills, continuing through a woods of cedars, oaks, and pines. Keep an eye out for trail plaques 12 and 13, which mark two different kinds of oak merged at the trunk. The black oak, on the right, has sharp, bristly leaves, while the white oak, on the left, has leaves with rounded lobes.

The trail soon crosses a paved bicycle path and then enters an area of black locust trees, easily identified by their thorns and compound leaves. The tree's brittle wood and shallow roots make it susceptible to strong winds and storms, and black locust is one of the first trees to topple during hurricanes.

Just before crossing the bike trail again, you'll see a small stand of trees of heaven. The intriguing name is a reference to the tree's fast-growing tendencies and tall height, as if reaching for the stars. The tree of heaven, native to Asia, thrives in waste areas and near as-

A scenic view of Salt Pond welcomes visitors at the start
of the Nauset Marsh Trail.

phalt roadways. It has a smooth trunk with pale gray bark, leaves that give off a rank odor when crushed, and winged, propeller-like seeds.

On the other side of the bike path, the Nauset Marsh Trail merges with the Buttonbush Trail. This unique, ¼-mile loop has interpretive plaques written in Braille as well as roman lettering and a rope handrail to guide the visually impaired. Turn right on the loop, and a few minutes along, the trail crosses a boardwalk above a small kettle pond where there's a good chance of spotting red-winged blackbirds. Scores of these colorful birds return each spring to build nests in the buttonbush shrubs that thrive in the pond's shallow waters. When you come to a fork, proceed to the right, and you'll shortly be back at the amphitheater.

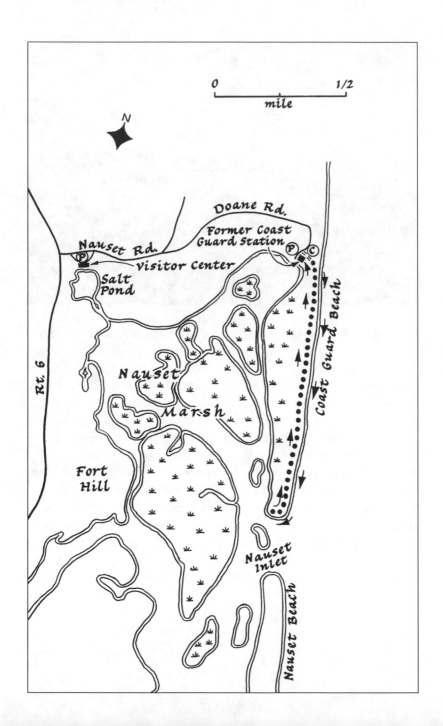

Coast Guard Beach

A walk along the barrier beach where naturalist Henry Beston wrote *The Outermost House,* and a chance to see wintering seals

Hiking distance: 2 miles
Hiking time: 1 hour

Coast Guard Beach, at the Cape Cod National Seashore, is a popular bathing beach in the summer, but the best time for doing this hike is November to May. Then it's a perfect beach for strolling, devoid of sunbathers and with plenty of space in the parking lot. Best of all, during those months you can often find wintering harbor seals sunning themselves on the shoals that emerge at low tide in Nauset Inlet, at the south end of Coast Guard Beach. Not only do the seals sun here, but they feed here as well. Salt marshes, like the expansive Nauset Marsh that backs Coast Guard Beach, are nurseries for sand eels, the seals' favorite food.

Harbor seals, which are relatively small, brownish seals with catlike whiskers and large liquid eyes, were once common, year-round residents on Cape Cod. Around the turn of the century, however, authorities concerned that "fish-eating seals" were depleting the local catch placed a bounty on seals—or, more specifically, on seal noses, which had the same effect. By about 1910, those seals that had escaped the bounty hunters had retreated northward.

Now protected by the Marine Mammal Protection Act of 1972, seals are returning in increasing numbers to the Cape. Not only have the relatively common harbor seals recolonized, but in recent years, less common gray seals have also reestablished breeding colonies. In addition to the year-round residents, thousands of other seals migrate south from Maine and Canada to winter on Cape Cod, easing the competition for fish up north during the lean, cold-weather months.

Seals do not always haul out at the same sites each day, but the chances of seeing them in winter on this walk are good if you go at low tide when the sandbars emerge. To pick the right time, call the National Seashore's Salt Pond Visitor Center at 508-255-3421 to check on both the tide table and recent seal sightings.

Coast Guard Beach has a rich human history as well. Before the Cape Cod Canal was completed in 1914, shifting shoals along the Outer Cape were a constant hazard to ships passing between Boston and points south. In 1872, the federal government formed the U.S. Life-Saving Service to aid vessels in distress, and this beach was selected as the site of one of nine stations built on the Outer Cape. Eventually the service developed into the U.S. Coast Guard, hence the beach's name.

In 1927, naturalist Henry Beston spent a year of solitude on Coast Guard Beach in a small, two-room cottage he built behind the dunes, sandwiched in the wild spaces between Nauset Marsh and the open Atlantic. Beston's recording of the seasonal changes and his interaction with the environment became the basis for his book *The Outermost House,* a chronicle that remains a classic in the field of American naturalist writings.

Although Beston left his legacy in print, the records of others who predated him were more recently unearthed. In November 1990, after a series of early-winter storms caused extensive erosion in the cliffs along Coast Guard Beach, an amateur archaeologist strolling along the beach discovered an ancient hearth at the high-tide line. A few days later, a U.S. National Park Service archaeological team began a salvage operation, hoping to excavate the site before the next storm washed more of the cliff away. Over the next month, they uncovered what turned out to be the oldest undisturbed archaeological site yet discovered in New England.

The excavation uncovered evidence of habitation from several different periods, including the Early Archaic Culture, dating back as far as eleven thousand years, and the more recent Woodland Culture of one thousand years ago. The earliest settlers were hunters and gatherers, who probably selected the site as a winter camp because of its protected inland location—for ten thousand years ago, the land that is now Coast Guard Beach was 5 miles away from the sea.

Access

Coast Guard Beach is 2 miles east of Route 6 in Eastham. To get there, turn onto Nauset Road at the entrance to the Salt Pond Visitor Center. When the road forks, take Doane Road, the road to the right. Upon reaching the coast, turn right onto the short drive to the old Coast Guard station.

In the summer, when the number of parking spaces is insufficient, beach visitors must park their cars at the Little Creek parking area on Doane Road, 1 mile past the Salt Pond Visitor Center, pay a parking fee, and take the seashore's shuttle bus down to the beach. Cyclists may use the bicycle racks at the beach year-round without fees.

Trail

Begin at the former Nauset Coast Guard Station, a handsome house of white clapboards and red roof at the edge of the headland overlooking Coast Guard Beach and Nauset Marsh. The station, built in 1936 and decommissioned in 1958, now serves as the Environmental Education Center for the National Seashore.

Follow the asphalt driveway down between the station and the former boathouse, which now serves as a bathhouse with rest rooms, showers, and a telephone. This driveway once led to a huge beachside parking lot until the infamous winter storm of 1978 wiped out the entire parking lot, two bathhouses, and much of the beach's barrier dunes in one fell swoop. The only remaining traces are chunks of asphalt that lie exposed on the sands during winter low tides, only to be reburied each year by the accumulation of summer sand.

Take a few minutes to read the four interesting interpretive plaques, one of which details the beach as it was before the big storm. The others discuss the Pilgrim landing, Coast Guard rescue missions, and Henry Beston's cottage, the remnants of which were washed away in 1978.

Then walk down the path to the beach and turn right. Most of the year, the sand is fairly well packed and easy to walk on and is

Harbor seals bask in the sun on the sandbars in Nauset Inlet.

lightly strewn with strands of rockweed, a green seaweed with air bladders.

The grass-covered sand dunes backing the beach are fenced off to protect the nesting sites of piping plovers, common terns, and least terns. The plovers can be spotted from early April and the terns arrive shortly thereafter. The chubby little plovers are as pale as the sand, giving them a natural camouflage that makes them tricky to spot. Keep an eye out for movement around the base of the dunes or for a small solitary figure scurrying up from the water's edge.

Because of the curve of the coastline, you won't be able to see seals until you've walked to the end of Coast Guard Beach, about 20 minutes away. When seals are present, you'll usually find them hauled out on the sandbars that emerge a few hundred feet offshore in Nauset Inlet.

Harbor seals are curious about people and will watch you watching them, but they're also quite skittish. A motorboat near the inlet can be enough to startle the seals back into the water.

If you don't see seals on the sandbars, look for them in the water, where they may be "bottling," that is, floating quietly with just their snouts pointing up. At any rate, the marsh views here are quite attractive, and the walk will not have been for naught, even if you don't spot seals.

On the opposite side of Nauset Inlet is Nauset Beach, another spot sometimes used by sunbathing harbor seals. Nauset Beach is part of Cape Cod National Seashore but managed by the town of Orleans.

Finish the walk by retracing your path back up the beach.

Wellfleet Bay Wildlife Sanctuary

A Massachusetts Audubon Society sanctuary with excellent birding

Hiking distance: 1½ miles
Hiking time: 1½ hours

The Massachusetts Audubon Society's Wellfleet Bay Wildlife Sanctuary encompasses nearly 800 acres of woods, salt marshes, ponds, fields, and heathlands. This varied habitat supports a large diversity of plants and animals and is a favorite locale for birders.

About 250 species of birds have been sighted at the sanctuary. Of those, some 60 are nesters, including the green heron, clapper rail, red-tailed hawk, northern harrier, American kestrel, screech owl, great horned owl, American woodcock, black-billed cuckoo, ruby-throated hummingbird, and prairie, pine, and yellow warblers.

The Massachusetts Audubon Society has owned and maintained the property since 1958. For three decades before that, it was the Austin Ornithological Research Station, a family-run bird-banding and research center. The station was the first place in the United States to use mist nets to catch birds for banding, now the standard throughout the country.

The sanctuary has more than 5 miles of hiking trails. Here we describe the Goose Pond Trail, an easy, mostly level, 1½-mile walk that starts in woodland, passes ponds, skirts a marsh, and returns over rolling heathland. Depending on tidal conditions, you can usually opt to add another mile onto the hike by crossing the marsh, making a loop around Try Island, and walking out to Cape Cod Bay. Waterproof footwear is recommended for the Try Island excursion.

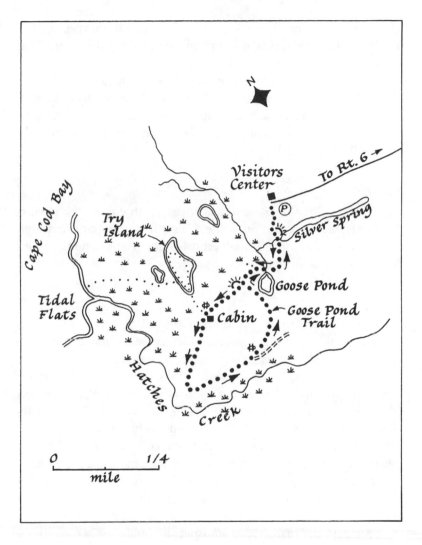

Entrance to the Wellfleet Bay Wildlife Sanctuary is free for Massachusetts Audubon Society members. Admission for nonmembers is $3 for adults, $2 for senior citizens and children. The sanctuary trails are open from 8 AM to 8 PM in summer, and from 8 AM to dusk the rest of the year. The visitors center has displays on flora and fauna, a bird-viewing room, and rest rooms. The center's gift shop sells birding and nature guides, including a useful, inexpensive trail guide that identifies 70 trees and plants found along the Goose Pond Trail.

The sanctuary's ongoing programs include nature walks, workshops, Monomoy Island tours, seal cruises, and canoe trips. In summer, there's also a natural history day camp for children and camping facilities for members. For more information, call the sanctuary at 508-349-2615.

Access

Wellfleet Bay Wildlife Sanctuary is at the south end of the town of Wellfleet. Heading north on Route 6, turn left at the sanctuary sign, 0.3 mile past the Eastham/Wellfleet town line. The sanctuary parking lot is 0.4 mile from Route 6.

Trail

The Goose Pond Trail begins south of the visitors center. Take a moment to admire the center's garden, which contains labeled plants that have been specifically selected to attract butterflies.

From the trailhead, the path winds down through a mixed woods of pine and oak to an earthen dam at the edge of a salt marsh. The pond on the left is Silver Spring, which until 1929, when the dam was built, was a brook that flowed freely across the marsh to Cape Cod Bay. The freshwater pond was created to expand the diversity of habitats on the property and attract more species of birds. Just before crossing the dam, take the short spur path on the left to the pond's edge, where you can often find painted turtles sunning on a nearby log. You're less apt to see the pond's snapping turtles, which cruise underwater snapping up unsuspecting bullfrogs. In summer, the pond becomes a garden of yellow and white water lilies, while red-blossomed cardinal flowers, which attract hummingbirds, bloom along the shore.

As you walk over the dam, there's an open view of the marsh, where narrow-leaved cattails and other reeds provide a favored habitat for red-winged blackbirds.

The trail then enters a mixed conifer woodland of Norway

spruce, red pine, Scotch pine, and white pine, some of the four thousand evergreens planted by the Austins. Before 1928, the property was a turnip and asparagus farm and was virtually treeless. The woods is a good place to look for pine warblers and chickadees, as well as the orange flash of the northern oriole or even a scarlet tanager.

After a few minutes, the trail curves to the right and leads over the earthen dike that separates Goose Pond from the salt marsh. This is one of the best birding spots along the trail, since the water in the pond is regulated throughout the year to attract different species. In late fall the pond is dammed, allowing it to collect winter's snow and rain, which gradually turns it into a freshwater pond attractive to ducks. In spring, Goose Pond is a good place to see black duck ducklings. About the second week in July, the sanctuary staff begins to lower the water level to expose mudflats around the edges, and the pond gradually becomes more tidal and brackish. During the summer and fall migration, shorebirds stop here to feed.

The tall, feathery phragmite reeds found in the pond are an attractive, though undesirable and invasive, grass that can easily tolerate Goose Pond's confused water regimes. Cattails are here as well, but the water is too salty for them to dominate.

After the trail crosses the dike, there are a few side paths on the right that lead through thickets to the edge of the marsh, a good place to spot snowy egrets, sandpipers, greater yellowlegs, and other shorebirds feeding in the salt-marsh tidal pools.

In a few minutes, the trail forks and starts the loop section of this route. Stay to the right, and you'll soon come to a wooden platform with a wide open view of the marsh. The wooded marsh island that you see directly ahead is Try Island, which, during Wellfleet's shore whaling era, was the site of a tryworks where whale blubber was boiled down to make oil.

The trail continues through a blanket of bearberry, which thrives in the dry sands just above the marsh, and soon comes to a bench opposite an old cabin. Here the side trail to Try Island leads off to the right. Unless the tide is unusually high, at which time the entire marsh floods, it's possible to walk out to and around Try Island and, from there, to cross a boardwalk to Cape Cod Bay.

Try Island is the last place on the Lower Cape to have an oak-

This trailside platform offers an ideal vantage point for spotting shorebirds.

hickory woodland, a type of habitat that was common when the Pilgrims landed. At high tide, the northeast side of the island is a good place to spot herons: great blue herons, little blue herons, great egrets, snowy egrets, and yellow-crowned and black-crowned night herons. The boardwalk leads to expansive tidal flats, where shorebirds feed. Birding is especially good around high tide, when the birds get pushed up closer to the boardwalk.

Whether or not you take the Try Island loop, continue on the main trail as it passes the cabin and heads west. Thickets of beach plum line the left side of the trail, while the right side is dotted with sea lavender and glasswort. You can sometimes find deer tracks in the marsh mud here, as well as small prints from other marsh visitors.

About 10 minutes beyond the cabin, the trail turns left and goes through a grove of black locust trees, easily identified by the sharp, thick thorns on the newer branches. Black locust, a native of the southern United States, was introduced to Cape Cod to help stem erosion. A member of the legume family, the seeds of the tree are eaten by pheasant, bobwhite, and deer.

The trail continues along a dirt vehicle road, with the marsh on the right and sloping heathlands on the left. Look in the marsh-side thickets for northern mockingbirds, easily identified in flight by the white patches on their wings.

At the trail sign, turn left off the main road and walk up into the heathlands. Plants that thrive in impoverished soils grow here: poverty grass, bearberry, bayberry, beach plum, and fragrant sweet fern. In fall, the asters that bloom in the fields attract migrating monarch butterflies.

After crossing the uplands, the trail comes back to Goose Pond, finishing the loop. Go back around the pond, retracing your steps through the woods, past Silver Spring, and back to the parking lot.

Atlantic White Cedar Swamp Trail

A delightful trail on an elevated boardwalk through a shady white cedar swamp

Hiking distance: 1¼ miles
Hiking time: 1 hour

There are just a few pockets of Atlantic white cedar on Cape Cod, including this one in the Cape Cod National Seashore. The Atlantic white cedar (also called southern white cedar) grows primarily in coastal swamps and bogs, most often in climates warmer than that of Massachusetts. It was probably introduced to the Cape during one of the periodic warming trends that have taken place over the past two thousand years.

Thanks to a well-constructed boardwalk over the spongy ground, visitors can walk into the midst of this white cedar swamp, an ecosystem that elsewhere is most commonly viewed from the sidelines. It's a very lovely walk, peaceful and shady.

White cedar is an attractive, aromatic evergreen. The bark is soft and somewhat loose and stringy, reddish brown in color and streaked with gray on the outermost layer. The wood is light and resistant to decay, good for lumber, boxes, fence posts, and, because it is resonant, pipe organs. The early English settlers favored white cedar in the construction of their homes and logged virtually every tree. Still, once having taken root, the Atlantic white cedar thrives in swamps, and eventually new trees sprouted.

The peat in the swamp has accumulated to a depth of 7 feet and supports a variety of understory plants. One that flourishes

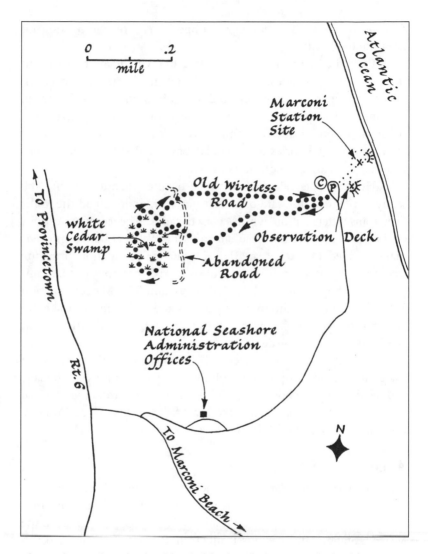

along the trail is the highbush blueberry. In August, the berries are ripe for the picking. Although the National Seashore prohibits the removal of other types of vegetation, fruit may be picked and eaten—so enjoy.

Before or after the hike, take in the expansive ocean views from the pavilion at the Marconi Station Site and from the observation deck on the bluff. Both are at the opposite end of the parking lot from the trailhead.

From the Marconi Station Site in 1903, Guglielmo Marconi, an Italian inventor, broadcast Morse code telegraph messages between President Theodore Roosevelt and King Edward VII in Cornwall, England. It was the first two-way wireless communication across the Atlantic. Within a matter of months, Americans and Europeans were exchanging news stories on a regular basis, and ship-to-shore communications had become commonplace.

However, the relentless advance of the Atlantic, eroding the sandy sea cliffs at the rate of 3 feet per year, undermined the Wellfleet transmitter station within two decades. The communications equipment was moved to Chatham, and the Wellfleet buildings eventually washed into the sea. Bits of concrete foundation from the transmitter house and from one of the 210-foot towers that supported the huge antenna are all that remain. The Marconi Station Site exhibit includes interpretive plaques and a diorama of the original transmitter house, towers, and antenna. Eventually the exhibit site itself will erode away.

From the observation deck, which stands a bit higher than the Marconi pavilion, it's possible to look across the width of the Cape and see the water on both sides. This stretch of land from the Marconi Station Site on the open Atlantic to Blackfish Creek on Cape Cod Bay is the narrowest part of Cape Cod, just 1 mile across.

Access

From the Cape Cod National Seashore's Salt Pond Visitor Center in Eastham, go 5 miles north on Route 6 to South Wellfleet and turn right at the traffic light into the Marconi Area. Follow the signs to the Marconi Station Site, which is 1 mile from Route 6. Park in the paved lot at the end of the road. There are rest rooms at the parking lot.

Trail

The National Seashore rates the Atlantic White Cedar Swamp Trail as a hike of "moderate difficulty" because of some log-reinforced steps and a half-mile walk through somewhat soft sand. The trailhead is clearly marked on the west side of the parking lot. Free brochures available here explain cedar swamp ecology.

The packed dirt trail is easy to follow, covered in places with wood chips or pine needles. Shortly beyond the trailhead, the trail leads off to the left through a dry, scrubby woods of pitch pine and bear oak. The trees are low and stunted, some twisted with curves and kinks, looking almost like overgrown bonsai. Small plaques point out black huckleberry and broom crowberry, both low-growing heaths that tolerate poor, sandy soil.

As you move inland away from the salt-laden winds of the coast, the trees grow taller and straighter. Closer to the swamp, the richer soil holds more moisture and supports lusher vegetation. In this area, you'll find black oaks, white oaks, and red maples.

Wintergreen, also called checkerberry or teaberry, is one of the ground-cover plants along the trail. When crushed, its aromatic leaves smell just like wintergreen candy. Early spring brings the fragrant, pale pink blossoms of the mayflower, the official state flower of Massachusetts. In summer, the bright pink flowers of the sheep laurel and the sticky white flowers of the swamp honeysuckle bloom. All these—as well as the blueberries—are members of the heath family, a group of shrubs and woody perennials that thrive in acidic soils.

After about 15 minutes, the path crosses an abandoned dirt road and makes a slight jog to the right. Follow the trail sign that marks the path to the boardwalk.

The wooden boardwalk circles through the white cedar swamp, passing over patches of plush green mosses and puddles of standing water. The woods are thick with tall, stately cedars that allow in only filtered light. Many of the trees have a pale green sheen from the bits of lichen growing on their bark. It all gives the sense of entering a primordial forest.

Go left at the first fork on the boardwalk, and then later bear left again at the second fork. This route will make a near-loop, omitting just a small segment of boardwalk. (It takes just 2 minutes to stroll down it if you're curious.) There are benches to sit on, although in summer the mosquitoes can get a bit pesky if you linger too long.

After leaving the boardwalk, the trail ends with a 10-minute

A winding boardwalk provides hiker access to this unique white cedar swamp.

walk along the sandy Old Wireless Road, which once led to the former wireless station. This segment of the trail is dry and unshaded and, though called a road, is accessible only to hikers.

The Old Wireless Road is edged much of the way with low-growing bearberry, which has shiny green leaves and red berries, and smaller patches of fragrant sweet fern. Note that the trees once again become stunted as you get closer to the coast.

Near the trail's end, just before the trailhead bench, you'll find bayberry bushes on the right side of the path. The early colonists harvested the waxy berries in the fall and used them to make candles.

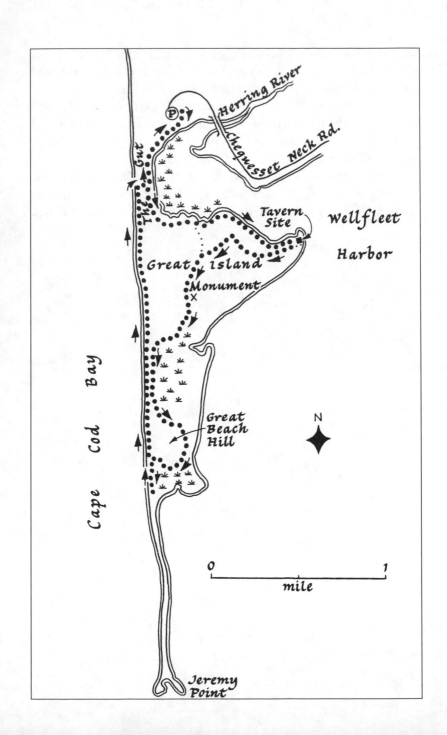

Great Island Trail

A hike down a long peninsula through marshland, dunes, and pine woods, returning along the beach

Hiking distance: 7 miles
Hiking time: 4 hours

Great Island Trail is the longest trail in the Cape Cod National Seashore and the farthest off the beaten path. This peaceful coastal hike is moderately strenuous, primarily due to some sections of soft sand.

Although it is now a peninsula, Great Island was, until 1831, a separate island off the southwest tip of Wellfleet. Great Beach Hill, which is connected to the south side of Great Island, also once stood alone. Over time, the forces of erosion and accretion built up sandbars between the islands, until eventually the islands were connected to each other and to the mainland. With the flow of water cut off between Wellfleet Harbor and Cape Cod Bay, extensive marshes built up along the eastern side of the new peninsula.

While Great Island today is an uninhabited wilderness area, it was once a bustling center for shore whalers. During precolonial times, the waters surrounding Wellfleet were frequented by migratory right whales and large pods of pilot whales. In the late 1600s, Wellfleet's early colonists began organizing whale hunts—a profitable venture since whale oil, which was used for lighting and lubrication, was a most prized commodity in the colonies, bringing as much as $60 a gallon. Lookout towers were built along the shores of Great Island, and, when whales were spotted, they were corralled by small boats and chased ashore for slaughtering. Dozens of pilot whales could be beached in a single hunt.

The early 1700s witnessed the heyday of activity on Great

Island—there was even a boisterous tavern where whalers stayed high, if not dry, while waiting for the sentry's call. In 1970, the site of the Smith Tavern was identified on a bluff at the northeast point of Great Island and was excavated by archaeologists from the National Park Service and Plimoth Plantation. Thousands of artifacts were unearthed, including clay pipe stems, pieces of mugs and ladies' fans, a 1724 farthing, and a large whale vertebra used as a chopping block.

When the first colonists arrived in Wellfleet, Great Island was covered with a dense hardwood forest. The settlers cut many of the trees to build houses and boats and used most of the rest as fuel to boil down whale blubber. After shore whaling died out, the largely denuded island was used for grazing animals and for harvesting oysters, the crushed shells of which were burned to make lime. The impact of all these activities resulted in serious erosion, and in the 1830s, pitch pines were planted in an effort to stabilize the soil.

The Great Island Trail crosses three kinds of terrain: the shady floors of the pine forests, tidal flats along the edge of the marshes, and sandy stretches along the dunes and beach. It's a good hike for spotting great blue herons, marsh hawks, scoters, eiders, mergansers, and even osprey.

Sunny spring and fall days are perfect for this hike. In winter, it can be cold and blustery, with winds lashing off the ocean, so bundle up. On hot summer days, take sunscreen, a sun hat, and plenty of water, as there are long stretches of open sun, and the white sands can reflect a lot of heat.

The hike will be most enjoyable if you start early and allow plenty of time. Consider bringing a picnic lunch to eat under the pines or along the beach. There's no water or facilities at the trailhead or along the way.

Access

From Route 6 in Wellfleet, turn west toward Wellfleet Center at the traffic lights, 5.2 miles north of the Eastham/Wellfleet town line. Take the first road to the left (which begins as East Commercial Street and ends as Chequesset Neck Road), and follow it 3.3 miles to its end. You'll pass the Wellfleet Harbor marina, where the road curves to the right, and cross the dike that spans Herring River before ending at the National Seashore's Great Island parking lot.

Trail

The hike begins at a marked trailhead on the east side of the parking lot and heads down through a pine forest to the edge of a marsh. The waterway to the left, out beyond the marsh, is the Herring River, which once cut clear across the area where you're standing and out to Cape Cod Bay. The narrow, sandy neck that now links Great Island to the rest of Wellfleet is called The Gut.

About 5 minutes down The Gut, there's a short boardwalk to the right that leads over grass-covered dunes to the beach and the open waters of Cape Cod Bay. It's worth the short climb both for the view and to see where the beach walk will connect back up to the trail on the return hike.

Once you reach the south end of The Gut, bear to the left and continue to skirt the marsh. You are now walking along the north side of Great Island. The hillside here is largely covered with bearberry, a member of the heath family that thrives in the sandy areas along the trail. This shiny, evergreen ground cover has white, bell-shaped flowers with pink tips that bloom in early May. In autumn, its bright red berries earn the plant its local nickname, hog cranberry. Although the berries are too mealy for most people, they are favored by the deer on Great Island. You'll also pass patches of trailside beach plum and bayberry. As you walk along the trail, look down to find tiny fiddler crabs scurrying about. These interesting creatures, the males distinguished by an oversized claw, actually change colors each day in sync with the tides.

After passing the cement posts from an old vehicle gate, the trail curves to the right and soon forks. The right fork, marked GREAT BEACH HILL, continues straight down the peninsula, and the left fork goes out to the site of the old Smith Tavern and then loops back to the main trail. If you were to take the right fork and bypass the loop, you'd cut about 45 minutes off the hike.

The 1⅓-mile loop that begins on the left is pleasant enough, but don't take it just to see the tavern site, as the site is unmarked and the excavation has been filled in. The walk does, however, skirt the south side of the marsh, providing a shoreline glimpse of marsh ecology. Odds are that among the flotsam and seashells, you'll find the brown, armorlike shells of horseshoe crabs washed up along the shore. Shortly before reaching the easternmost point of Great Island, the trail leaves the shore and climbs up across the dunes, where a spur to the left leads to a small beach on Wellfleet Harbor. The main route takes the right fork, which travels across a dense pine woods whose floor is covered with lichen and dotted with a variety of mushrooms. In about 20 minutes, when this trail merges back with the main trail, turn left and continue south through the pines.

After about 5 minutes along the main trail, look to the left for a small clearing where an engraved, granite monument has been placed by a descendant of William Bradford, a passenger on the *Mayflower* and the second governor of Plymouth colony. Five minutes farther, the trail comes out of the woods and out along the northwest side of the marsh between Great Island and Great Beach Hill. This marsh is an excellent place to spot great blue herons feeding, particularly at high tide. We've seen more than half a dozen in a single sighting.

When you get to the south end of the marsh, ignore the path that curves left, and instead take the trail straight ahead up through the sandy dunes, climbing Great Beach Hill. This section of the trail is one of the more strenuous because of its soft sands, though it becomes less sloggy as the pitch pine woods get thicker. It takes about 10 minutes to cross Great Beach Hill, which is followed by another marsh.

Once on the marsh, follow the trail that curves to the right, and you'll soon come to some sand flats that are emerged at low tide and flooded at high tide. These flats lead out across a thin peninsula to Jeremy Point, 1½ miles away. If you time your visit with the tides, it's possible to walk all the way to the end. In winter, with a scope or binoculars, you can sometimes see hundreds of harbor seals sunning themselves on sand spits off Jeremy Point (or on chunks of ice in the bay).

When you're ready to head back, follow the trail over the dunes and down to Cape Cod Bay. The walk north along the beach, which is the most direct way back to the trailhead, takes about an hour. It's a fine walking beach, much of it below eroding hills and low sand dunes, and an excellent place to find colorful scallop shells and to spot sea ducks and shorebirds. When you reach The Gut, take the boardwalk back over the dunes and retrace your steps back to the parking lot.

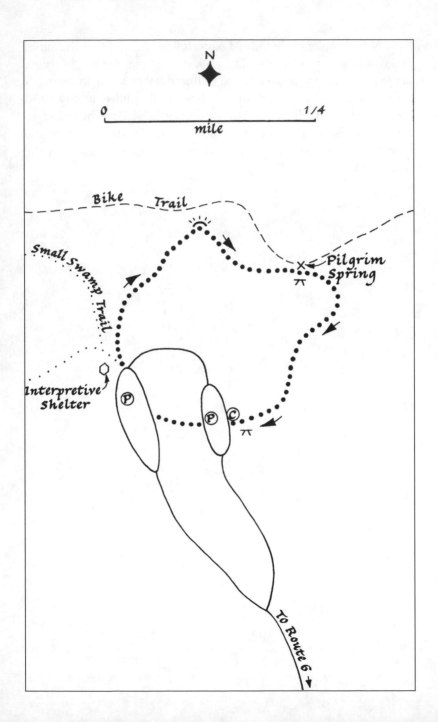

Pilgrim Spring Trail

A short walk to the site where the Pilgrims first found water in the New World

Hiking distance: ¾ mile
Hiking time: ½ hour

The Cape Cod National Seashore's Pilgrim Spring Trail leads to the spring where the Pilgrims found their first fresh water after arriving in New England.

At sunrise on November 11, 1620, the *Mayflower* dropped anchor in Provincetown Harbor, just inside the tip of Cape Cod. On board were 101 passengers who had endured meager rations and cramped quarters for 65 days at sea. The voyage from England had been arduous, and although the group had originally intended to reach the Hudson River and the Virginia colonies, they were grateful simply to have found a safe harbor in the New World.

There were complications, however. The charter they had been granted was valid only in the Virginia Colony, and some of the men were on the verge of mutiny. The Pilgrims therefore spent that first day at Provincetown in the cabin of their ship, where they drew up and signed the now-famous Mayflower Compact, in which they agreed to stay together and establish their own government.

The next day the men went ashore to gather firewood, and the women washed clothes using salt water from the bay. On the fourth day, Captain Miles Standish, who had been hired as the group's military officer, took 15 men armed with muskets and set out on a 3-day expedition. In addition to searching for food and water, they scouted the area to determine its suitability as a permanent settlement.

The expedition party came across a few Indians, who, not surprisingly, fled when they saw these foreign men with guns. Although they were unable to make contact with the Natives, the Englishmen did help themselves to several baskets of seed corn that they discovered stored in a place now known as Corn Hill.

But, most importantly, they found fresh water, pure and sweet. "We . . . sat us downe and drunke our first New England water with as much delight as ever we drunke drinke in all our lives," reported one of the men. A plaque marks the historic site, now called Pilgrim Spring.

After completing three expeditions around the Lower Cape, the Pilgrims decided not to stay on Cape Cod. In mid-December, with winter fast approaching, the *Mayflower* sailed west from Provincetown and landed at Plymouth Bay.

Access

The Pilgrim Spring Trail is off Route 6 in North Truro, 7.6 miles north of the Truro/Wellfleet town line. The turnoff is marked PILGRIM HEIGHTS, and the trailhead is at the parking lot 0.5 mile down the access road.

Trail

The Pilgrim Spring Trail starts at the interpretive shelter at the end of the parking lot, to the right of the trailhead for the Small Swamp Trail.

This walk is an easy loop, much of it through a thick, pitch pine woods that provides a soft cushion of pine needles underfoot. About 5 minutes from the trailhead, the path comes out of the trees to an open overlook at the edge of Salt Meadow Marsh, with views of the sand dunes and the distant ocean beyond.

This overlook is a good vantage point for spotting raptors that hunt for small rodents in the marsh below. Chances of sightings are best on warm, sunny days during the hawk migration of early spring. Sharp-shinned hawks and American kestrels are most commonly seen, but lucky hikers might also catch glimpses of northern harriers (also called marsh hawks) in courtship.

The landscape does not look the same now as it did when the

A trailside plaque marks the spot where the Pilgrims first found fresh water in the New World.

Pilgrims were here. In those days, a large brackish creek ran through the marsh, emptying west of this spot into East Harbor on Cape Cod Bay. In 1869, a dike built to bring the railroad to Provincetown cut the harbor off from the sea, and the marsh grasses began to spread and flourish. Water from the marsh now drains slowly into nearby Pilgrim Lake, which is all that remains of the former East Harbor.

Still, the meandering cut of water you see below roughly parallels the route the Pilgrims walked up, and it's easy to imagine the small band of armored men cautiously slogging their way through the marsh mud.

From the overlook, the trail heads back inland and down to the plaque marking the spot where the Pilgrims discovered the bubbling spring of fresh water. The date was November 16, 1620. The spring still flows, although rather unceremoniously through a pipe that has been stuck into the ground to enable the water to run more freely.

If you feel like taking a break, there is a picnic table at this spot. (The paved path you see here between the spring and the cattail patch is a bike trail that connects High Head Road with Head of the Meadow Beach.)

From the spring site, Pilgrim Spring Trail heads back through pine woods and out to another picnic area. Walk past the rest rooms and across the parking lots to get back to the interpretive shelter where the trail began.

Small Swamp Trail

A walk to scenic viewpoints
atop glacial headlands and
down into a kettle swamp

Hiking distance: ¼ mile
Hiking time: ½ hour

S mall Swamp Trail is an easy loop walk in the Cape Cod National Seashore's Pilgrim Heights area. There are slight to moderate slopes and log-reinforced earthen steps along the way.

After taking in marshland and ocean views, the Small Swamp Trail circles inside a kettle hole, formed by a huge block of ice left behind by a retreating glacier at the end of the last Ice Age, fifteen thousand years ago. The depression created by the block remained even after the ice had melted.

The "Small" in the trail name does not refer to the size of the swamp in the center of this glacial kettle but was the name of the 200-acre farm that once occupied the area. The farm was started in 1860 by Thomas Small, who grew corn and asparagus, raised cattle on salt-marsh hay, and planted apple and plum trees. Thomas's son, Warren, later took over the farm; but the land was not highly productive, and when Warren Small died in 1922, the farm was abandoned.

The Smalls were not the first to live on the land, nor were they the first to cultivate corn here. Core samples taken of the swamp peat contained traces of corn pollen in several layers, indicating settlements by American Indians dating back some four thousand years.

The trail is nice to walk in any season. In late spring, bearberry, beach plum, yellow-flowered beach heather, starflower, and false lily of the valley come into bloom. Summer adds greenery and still more flowering plants. The marshland retains shades of golds, russets, and

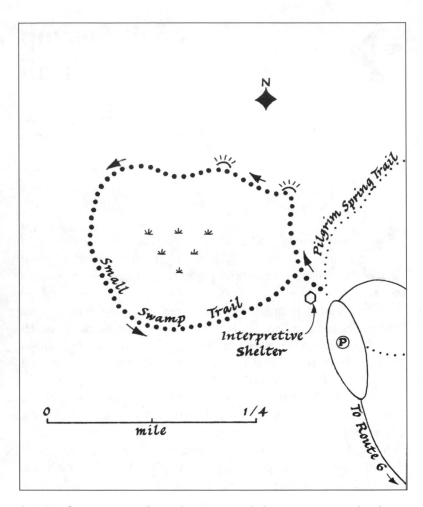

browns from autumn through spring, and the views across the dunes to the distant blue ocean are beautiful year-round.

Access

The Small Swamp Trail is off Route 6 in North Truro, 7.6 miles north of the Truro/Wellfleet town line. The turnoff is marked PILGRIM HEIGHTS and the trailhead is at the parking lot 0.5 mile down the access road.

The Small Swamp Trail offers views across Salt Meadow Marsh.

Trail

The trail, which starts at the interpretive shelter at the end of the parking lot, heads down through a woods of pitch pine. At the first fork, take the trail to the right. A few minutes from the trailhead, you'll come to the first of two viewpoints offering scenic vistas of marsh, dunes, and the Atlantic beyond. The viewpoints are on the edge of glacial headlands that were once whipped by open ocean. Then, about six thousand years ago, ocean currents began bringing up sand from the beaches of the Outer Cape, and gradually a sandy arm (now known as the Provincetown spit) began to develop about a half-mile offshore, paralleling the sea cliffs. Over time, the area between the newly emerging sand dunes and the former sea cliffs was sealed off from the open ocean and eventually became the marsh you see below.

After the second viewpoint, the trail leads down into the kettle hole, passing bearberry, bayberry, and blueberry before coming to a grove of quaking aspen trees. The bottom of this hollow, sheltered from the harsh coastal winds, is where Thomas Small built his farmhouse and barns. The buildings burned down long ago, however, and the only visible remains from that period are a few lilac bushes and fruit trees that survive in the tangled overgrowth.

A boardwalk over standing water is a reminder that Small Swamp is indeed a swamp, and here you can find Virginia rose, swamp azalea, sweet pepperbush, and other plants that love damp ground and acidic soil.

Just past the boardwalk, where both highbush and lowbush blueberries bear edible fruit in August, the trail climbs back up the wooded hill to the trailhead.

Beech Forest Trail

A trail through a beech forest, skirting freshwater ponds

Hiking distance: 1 mile
Hiking time: 45 minutes

This trail is in the Province Lands, the Cape Cod National Seashore area that bounds the village of Provincetown at the outermost tip of Cape Cod. The trail combines a mostly level, ¾-mile loop around freshwater ponds with a connecting ¼-mile loop that climbs up and down some moderate slopes through a forest of American beech trees.

The usual image of the Province Lands is one of sand dunes, open ocean, and endless shoreline. Yet this is not a beach trail but a beech trail—a beautiful little woodland oasis in the midst of the dunes.

Most of the Province Lands were heavily forested until European settlers began moving in around the mid-1600s. They cleared the land for homesteads and farming, used the lumber for houses and ships, and allowed animals to graze freely. It was an ecological disaster. Once the vegetation was lost, the Province Lands became little more than an unstable sand spit. With nothing to hold the soft beach sands in place when storm winds whipped off the ocean, the sands built up into shifting dunes. Sand drifts blew through Provincetown, burying streets, clogging up the harbor, and mounding around homes.

In response, the 1800s ushered in Cape Cod's first erosion-control projects, as Provincetown residents began replanting beach grass, shrubbery, and pines. These days, the people of Provincetown no longer have to worry about their homes, although some sections of

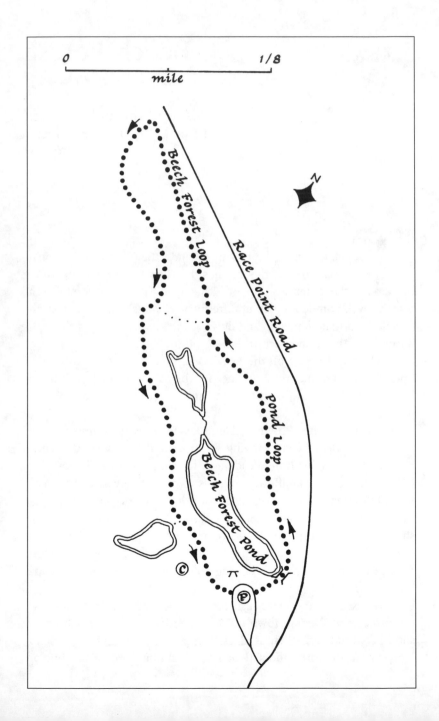

Route 6 that wind through the Province Lands must still be periodically plowed clear of drifting sand.

The Beech Forest is the only bit of hardwood forest left in the Province Lands, but even it is not virgin forest, having been completely cleared a century ago. Still, here in this mature woodland, one can get a sense of what all of Cape Cod must have looked like some three hundred years ago.

The Beech Forest Trail is a good walk in any season. It's cool and shady in midsummer when elsewhere in Provincetown the sun gleams hot off the white sands. In spring, mayflowers, false lilies of the valley, starflowers, and pink lady's slippers sprinkle the woodland floor.

Around the last two weeks of May, the Beech Forest is the best place on Cape Cod to see and hear tiny, colorful warblers as they migrate through in waves from Central America. About two dozen kinds of warblers stop here to rest on their way north, of which the yellow warbler, Blackburnian warbler, and the black-and-white warbler are most common. Dressed in their breeding plumage, the birds look like decorative ornaments atop spring's still-bare tree branches. The warblers also make an appearance during their fall migration, but at that time they're not as easy to spot.

Access

The Beech Forest Trail is in the Province Lands area of the Cape Cod National Seashore. Take Route 6 to Provincetown and turn right off the highway at the traffic lights onto Race Point Road. Turn left after 0.6 mile at the BEECH FOREST sign, and park in the large parking lot.

Trail

The Pond Loop begins at the right side of the parking lot. Start down the dirt path into the woods, and almost immediately you'll come to a little wooden footbridge overlooking Beech Forest Pond, one of the prettiest spots on the trail.

The golden club, an aquatic plant that is protected in Massachusetts, thrives in this pond. In May, its yellow spikes poke up out of

The starflower is a common spring wildflower.

the water by the thousands. In summer, the pond is chock-full of water lilies, their bold, white flowers with yellow centers sitting upon heart-shaped pads. Frogs harbored amongst the lily pads provide an audio backdrop to this lovely woodland setting.

The trail then passes over packed sand, where black oak is predominant, and softer sand, where pine trees thrive. Three kinds of pines are easily identified in these woods. Pitch pine, the Cape's most common pine tree, has stiff needles in tufts of three, sometimes growing directly out of the tree trunk. Austrian pine has long, shiny needles and Scotch pine has short, twisted needles; on both species the needles are in bundles of two.

Small plaques at points along the trail identify blueberries, black huckleberry, wild sarsaparilla, catbrier, bracken fern, checkerberry, swamp azalea, and poison ivy. You might also spot bayberry, shadbush, beach plum, and black cherry.

As you continue along the trail, the woods gets thicker and the beech trees more predominant. When you come to a trail crossing, continue straight ahead to begin the Beech Forest Loop. Here, the beech trees are so thick that only filtered light penetrates the treetops, and most ground-level greenery is limited to ferns and velvety mosses. Most beech leaves do not fall in autumn but, rather, dry to a golden brown and stay on the tree for quite a long time. In winter, the combination of golden leaves, smooth silver-gray tree trunks, and bright blue sky makes an attractive contrast.

After a few minutes along the Beech Forest Loop, the trail turns left, climbs up a log-reinforced stairway to the top of a knoll, and then winds back down to meet up again with the Pond Loop. This side of the Pond Loop is bordered by low hills, where a scramble to the top will bring you to the edge of a wide expanse of undulating sand dunes.

Farther down the Pond Loop, you'll pass a second body of water on the right side of the trail. Here, you can walk out onto a little wooden pier and gaze out over a shallow pond filled with frogs, grasses, and water lilies. At the edge of the pond, look for pickerelweed, an aquatic plant with spikes of purple flowers and heart-shaped leaves that end in a point.

The trail ends at the parking area shortly thereafter, where there are pond-side picnic tables.

Martha's Vineyard

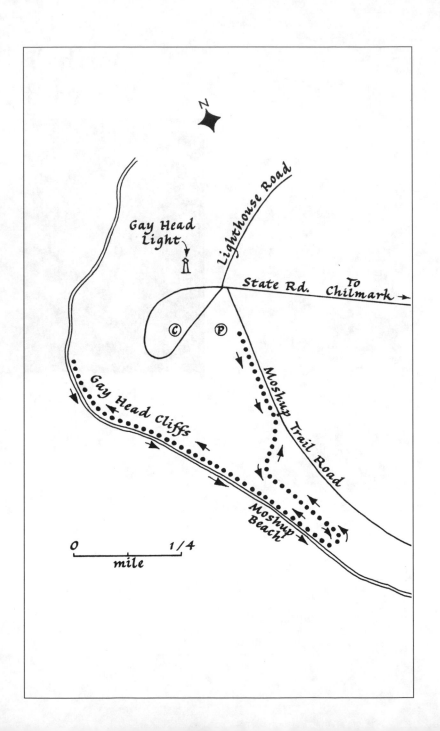

Gay Head Cliffs

A beach walk along the Vineyard's colorful Gay Head Cliffs

Hiking distance: About 3 miles,
depending on the tide
Hiking time: About 1½ hours

The spectacular Gay Head Cliffs, the most famous natural landmark on Martha's Vineyard, provide a colorful backdrop that makes this beach stroll truly unique.

The cliffs are formed of layers of clay and other sediments in hues of deep rose and salmon pink, mustard yellows, tawny browns, chalky whites, and deep grays. Eroded by wind and water, some of the cliffs are smooth and rounded, while others are sharp and jagged.

Although beautiful at any time of day, the optimal time to walk the beach is an hour or two before sunset when the rays of the setting sun reflect off the cliffs and heighten the colors. The trail to the base of the cliffs is under the jurisdiction of the Martha's Vineyard Land Bank Commission, which maintains 5 acres of ocean beach and 6 acres of cliff top, officially known as Moshup Beach and Moshup Beach Overlook.

The beach is named for the legendary Indian giant Moshup, who plays a prominent role in Vineyard folklore and is said to have lived at Gay Head in an area known as Devil's Den. Moshup reputedly had such a big appetite that he roasted whole whales for dinner atop a fire built of large trees, which he pulled up by the roots. Legend has it that the colorful Gay Head Cliffs were built from the mounds of garbage Moshup tossed from his home, the gray colors attributed to the ashes from his fires.

Moshup is also credited with creating the rock-covered shoals called Devil's Bridge that extend off Gay Head and have been responsible for scores of shipwrecks over the years. As the story goes, Moshup agreed to build a bridge from Gay Head to Cape Cod to make it easier for the Wampanoag Indians who lived on the Vineyard to trade with people on the mainland. A soothsayer told Moshup the bridge would have to be completed in a single night. An easy task, he thought, and after sunset on the next full moon he began laying stones on the sea floor. Before Moshup was halfway through, however, a large crab grabbed his toe, forcing the giant ashore to kick it off. While on land, Moshup took a nap and failed to awaken until sunrise, forever leaving the incomplete Devil's Bridge to catch unwary seafarers by surprise.

Long before the coming of the Ice Age, the land now known as Gay Head Cliffs was a section of coastal hills on the mainland. It is the oldest exposed land on all of Cape Cod and the Islands and is thought to be between 75 and 100 million years old.

The cliffs' variously colored layers were created during different geological epochs and contain fossils from their respective periods. The deep grays at the lower part of the cliffs are from prehistoric forests. The gravel near the top is from a later period and contains the remains of large ocean animals such as whales and sharks—even the partial skeleton of a camel has been unearthed.

Although, these days, digging into the cliffs is strictly forbidden, alert hikers may be fortunate enough to spot a shark's tooth or other such relic that has washed down from the cliffs onto the beach after a heavy storm.

In summer, Gay Head is heavily visited by sunbathers, and the northernmost end is a popular nude beach, despite posted signs to the contrary.

Access

The Gay Head Cliffs are in the town of Aquinnah (called Gay Head until 1998) at the westernmost point of the island. Take State Road all the way to its end, where it makes a loop.

Parking is at the town-owned lot at the intersection of State Road and Moshup Trail Road, where a fee of $15 per day is charged during the summer and on some off-season weekends. Cyclists may use the bicycle racks on the beach at no charge.

At the top of the loop, just beyond the lighthouse and below the complex of souvenir stores and snack shops, there is a smaller lot with free parking but with a time limit of only 1 hour. There are rest rooms between the two parking lots.

Trail

From the parking lot, it's a 10-minute walk down to the beach along a sandy trail that is partly covered by boardwalk and parallels the paved vehicle road known as Moshup Trail.

The view straight ahead is of Nomans Island, which lies 5 miles offshore. The island, which until 1996 was held by the U.S. military as a bombing target, is now managed by the U.S. Fish and Wildlife Service as a national wildlife refuge.

When you reach the beach, turn right to walk toward the cliffs. From here you can see the Elizabeth Islands, with Cuttyhunk at the southern end of the chain, which continues northeast to Naushon Island, just off Woods Hole.

Along the beach, a small section of grass-covered dunes soon gives way to the southern end of the Gay Head Cliffs. These coastal cliffs are striking. Each vivid color is the result of a different deposit in the clay. Some of the reddish tints are from deposits of iron oxide, for example, and the white clay is the result of high concentrations of kaolin and feldspar. Although still magnificent, the Gay Head Cliffs have suffered serious erosion over the years, and have lost some of their former grandeur.

For centuries, the Wampanoag Indians dug clay from the cliffs for making colorful pottery. Later, white settlers used Gay Head clay to build roads, paint their houses, and make bricks, the latter on a commercial scale for a brief period at the turn of the last century. Fossil hunters have torn away sections of cliff face looking for teeth and bones, and until quite recently, it was commonplace for beachgoers to play in the clay, painting their bodies in fanciful colors and then washing off in the sea. To preserve the cliffs, digging is now strictly prohibited, as is touching the cliff face or walking up on the clay.

The rich colors and formations of the clay cliffs glow in the afternoon light.

As you proceed northward along the beach, the cliffs come closer to the ocean edge. The tides will determine how far down you'll be able to walk; the last time we hiked here, we walked about a mile before we had to turn around and come back.

When you reach the end, retrace your steps back down the beach. As you walk, look up at the top of the sea cliffs to find the round holes made by bank swallows, which arrive on the Vineyard in mid-May and nest in colonies throughout the summer.

On the way back to the parking lot, Gay Head Light will be directly ahead. This attractive, circular, brick lighthouse was built in 1844. In 1856 it was fitted with a circular Fresnel lens consisting of 1,009 glass prisms that rotated around an oil lamp. As the glass passed in front of the light, it appeared to blink on and then off. After the light was electrified in 1952, the lens was moved to Edgartown, where it is now displayed on the grounds of the Martha's Vineyard Historical Society.

Cedar Tree Neck Sanctuary

A nature sanctuary with lovely woodland, pond, and coastal views

Hiking distance: 2½ miles
Hiking time: 2 hours

Cedar Tree Neck is a special place, offering one of the most attractive and varied hikes on the Vineyard. A network of trails leads through unspoiled woodlands, past freshwater ponds, across a bog, up onto sandy bluffs, and along a beach with views of the Elizabeth Islands and Cape Cod.

The 300-acre Cedar Tree Neck Sanctuary is the largest of nearly one hundred properties managed by the Sheriff's Meadow Foundation, an island-based conservation group that has been acquiring land preserves since 1959. The sanctuary encompasses Cedar Tree Neck, a rounded promontory that extends out into Vineyard Sound.

The sanctuary's 3½ miles of trails provide plenty of options for a very pleasant half-day outing. For those with limited time, several short trails loop out from the parking lot. The prettiest of these, the red trail, leads down to the beach in about 15 minutes. All the trails are marked and color-coded, and all are easy walking.

In spring and summer, you're apt to hear the calls of the towhee, wood thrush, ovenbird, and veery, all birds that nest in the sanctuary. A pair of ospreys that return each April to a nesting platform installed just outside the sanctuary can sometimes be spotted fishing in Cedar Tree Neck Pond. The sanctuary has lots of chipmunks and gray squirrels, and it's not unusual to spot white-tailed deer, especially on the yellow trail.

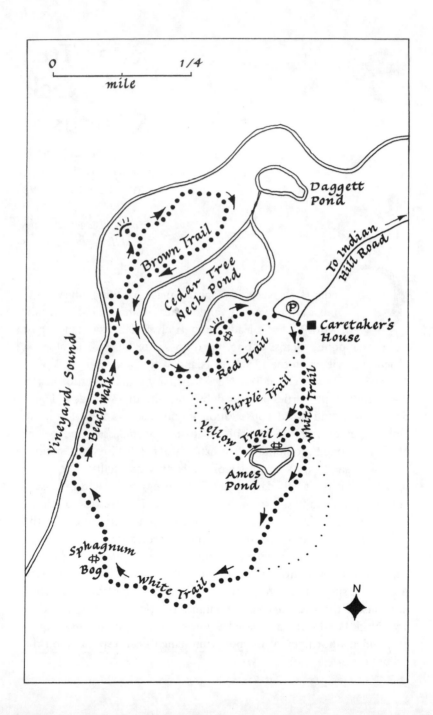

The Cedar Tree Neck Sanctuary is open daily 8:30–5:30. Picnicking and sunbathing are not allowed, and there are no rest rooms.

Access

From the intersection of State Road and Old County Road, at the north side of West Tisbury, take State Road 1.3 miles to the southwest and turn right onto Indian Hill Road. After 1.8 miles, turn right at the small sign for Cedar Tree Neck. Follow the signs into the sanctuary exactly 1 mile along a bumpy, winding dirt road. Turn left into the parking lot at the sign that reads OBED SHERMAN DAGGETT AND MARIA ROBERTS DAGGETT SANCTUARY, the official (but seldom-used) name for the Cedar Tree Neck Sanctuary.

Trail

Start on the white trail, which begins between the caretaker's house and the trail map signboard. The path leads through a mixed woods, dominated by oaks and sassafras. Sassafras is easy to identify by its leaves, which come in distinct one-lobe, two-lobe, and three-lobe shapes on the same branch; the two-lobe leaf is shaped like a mitten.

After a few minutes, the purple trail joins the white trail on the right. Stay on the white trail, which soon passes a stand of red pines on the left. Then, a few minutes later, turn right onto the yellow trail.

Maple and beech trees join up with oaks along this segment of the trail. In a couple of minutes, Ames Pond appears, where a wooden bench invites you to sit and take in the view. This pretty little pond is surrounded by maples and beetlebung trees. Beetlebung is the name used on the Vineyard for the tupelo (sour gum) tree, which has oval leaves that turn a brilliant red in autumn.

Ames Pond provides habitat for spring peepers, small tree frogs that make a loud, shrill call in early spring; painted turtles, which can often be found sunning themselves on logs in the water; and green frogs, snapping turtles, and muskrats.

If you want to see more of the pond, you can follow the yellow trail to its western side. Either way, you'll then need to backtrack to the intersection of the white and yellow trails. Turn right on the white trail and follow it uphill, catching peeks of the ocean through the woods along the way.

The trail then leads down to a sphagnum bog, which is spanned by a little boardwalk bridge with a bench. Pause for a moment to look around. This wet lowlands area is punctuated by swamp maples that turn bright red in autumn. At the edge of the bridge is a huge beech tree with ropelike roots that snake up through a bed of velvety green moss, creating an intricate design of nature's own artwork.

After the bog, the trail goes up a sandy cliff and then down again, coming out at the beach in about 5 minutes. From here, you get a clear view of the Elizabeth Islands.

Turn right and walk north along the beach for about 10 minutes. The beach, which changes with the seasons, is primarily large pebbles in the winter and white sand in the summer. Sometimes pieces of shipwrecks wash up on shore. The dunes that back the beach are covered with pasture rose, bayberry, sweet gale, and other coastal shrubs.

Keep an eye out for two rather inconspicuous color-coded posts at the edge of the vegetation line, the first of which leads up to the red trail, the second to the brown trail. Turn right at the second post, just before the point, and follow the brown trail inland where it makes a half-mile loop. Take the path to the left to walk the loop in a clockwise direction.

After just a few minutes, you'll come to a little spur trail to the left that leads up to a bluff with a wonderful panoramic view of Vineyard Sound. From here you can see up and down the coast and across to Woods Hole on Cape Cod.

The brown trail continues around the promontory, offering more coastal views, and then loops back, skirting Cedar Tree Neck Pond. The neck is named for the eastern red cedar trees found in this area.

Along the pond, the trail passes through a grove of sassafras trees that provide a near canopy effect, their snaky trunks stunted from blasts of salt wind.

At the end of the loop, take the same route back to the beach and walk south until you reach the red post, where you'll turn inland

*The wood anemone is a lovely spring wildflower found
in the woodlands of Martha's Vineyard.*

onto the red trail. Along the way you'll find a nice view across the pond to the old Daggett homestead, a private residence just outside the sanctuary boundaries.

Long ago, Cedar Tree Neck Pond was worked as a cranberry bog, and Ames Pond was created to serve as a water reservoir for flooding the bog at harvesttime. The crimson red berries that bobbed up after the bog was flooded were then gathered from the surface of the water.

Continue on the red trail, first crossing a little stream and then bearing left where the yellow trail comes in on the right. Shortly after this junction, the red trail will fork. Take the path to the left, down toward Cedar Tree Neck Pond. You'll soon come to a stone bench on a slope that's perfect for contemplating the view across the pond and dunes and out to the Elizabeth Islands. This overlook provides one of the loveliest views in the sanctuary.

The red trail then leads across a brook and back to the parking lot, a 2-minute walk from the stone bench.

Waskosims Rock Reservation

A peaceful walk through one of the largest undisturbed areas on the Vineyard

Hiking distance: 2½ miles
Hiking time: 1½ hours

Waskosims Rock Reservation, in the midst of the Mill Brook Valley, is named for an impressive ridge-top boulder that has played an important role in Wampanoag Indian history and legend. The trail passes by the huge rock, winds through woodlands and clearings, leads past old stone walls, and meanders alongside the serene waters of Mill Brook. It also offers a panoramic view from one of the highest hills on the island.

The original 145 acres of the 185-acre reservation were purchased in 1990 for $3.5 million by the Martha's Vineyard Land Bank Commission, culminating a long struggle led by the Vineyard Conservation Society to protect the area from development. The land bank, which seeks to preserve the island's rural landscape and environmentally sensitive areas, is funded by a 2 percent tax levied on Martha's Vineyard real estate transactions.

Waskosims Rock Reservation protects a number of rare plants, including the cranefly orchid, an endangered species. The Vineyard is the only place remaining in New England where the orchid is known to exist, and its recent discovery near Waskosims Rock played an important role in setting this property aside for conservation.

Other rare plants include the bushy rockrose, green wood orchid, LeConte's violet, golden saxifrage, poke milkweed, hooked crowfoot, sandplain flax, southern lady fern, long beech fern, and running clubmoss. The American brook lamprey, an eel-like fish no

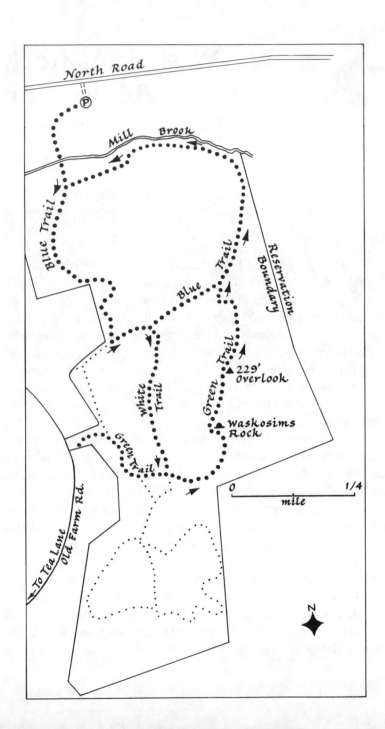

longer found anywhere else in the state because of its extreme sensitivity to minute levels of pollution, still swims in the pristine waters of Mill Brook.

The reservation is also home to the northern parula, a wood warbler with a yellow throat and blue-gray back that builds its nests out of old-man's-beard, a type of threadlike, hanging lichen found in the reservation's damp woodlands. Although the northern parula commonly migrates through the area in May, it is thought that fewer than two dozen pairs nest in all of Massachusetts.

Although few hikers will chance upon these rare species, the reservation's quiet spaces, sweeping vistas, and historic Waskosims Rock are easily accessible to all.

Access

Access is on North Road, just southwest of the West Tisbury–Chilmark town line and 0.4 mile northeast of Old Farm Road. A parking lot, a bicycle rack, and an information board are at the trailhead, but there are no other facilities.

Deer hunting is allowed on the property for one week each year, usually around Thanksgiving, and the reservation is posted and closed to hikers at that time. For information, call the Martha's Vineyard Land Bank Commission at 508-627-7141.

Trail

The trails in Waskosims Rock Reservation are well maintained and clearly marked with color-coded blazes. There are some modest hills, but the walk is not strenuous.

We combine three trails. The walk starts on the blue trail at the south side of the parking lot, connects after ¾ mile to the white trail, and loops back to the blue trail via the green trail. Although the route may sound a bit complicated, it's actually quite easy to follow.

The blue trail cuts through predominantly oak woodlands, with a smattering of beech trees and highbush blueberries. A couple of minutes after leaving the trailhead, you'll cross picturesque Mill Brook and shortly thereafter reach the blue trail's main loop.

Continue south, taking the loop in a counterclockwise direction.

Waskosims Rock is not only the most prominent landmark along this trail but also the source of many Indian legends.

You'll pass an old stone fence, the first of many that remain witness to the homesteads that stood here in colonial times. If you look closely, you'll also notice once-domestic apple trees amongst the thick brush beside the wall. About 5 minutes beyond this, you'll reach a T-junction at an old carriage road posted with a #33 marker. Turn left, and continue until you reach the white trail.

Bear right onto the white trail, which heads south across a meadow. After about 5 minutes, a spur of the green trail crosses the white trail, but don't take it—instead, continue south on the white trail until you reach marker #34, where the lower end of the green trail comes in. Turn left onto the green trail at the marker.

After about 5 minutes on the green trail, you'll come to Waskosims Rock, a huge boulder split diagonally from top to bottom. This rock is one of the many glacial erratics carried down from the north by the Wisconsin ice sheet some twenty thousand years ago. The native Wampanoag Indians, who saw in it the likeness of the head of a breaching whale, named the rock Waskosims, or "whale turned to stone." This image is especially striking from the path around the rock's narrower front side.

The boulder marks the boundary of the towns of Chilmark and West Tisbury. In days past, it was used by local Indian chiefs as a boundary for dividing their lands and in the 1600s as a marker for lands sold to white settlers. Legends denote the rock as a place of refuge and sanctuary.

A few minutes beyond Waskosims Rock, the trail reaches an elevation of 229 feet, one of the highest points on the Vineyard. From here there's a sweeping 180-degree view across the island, and on a clear day you can see the Vineyard Haven water tower 7 miles to the northeast.

From this summit, you can appreciate just how rural Martha's Vineyard really is. Other than the distant water tower and a farmhouse on Fisher Pond in the Mill Brook Valley below, there's virtually no development to be seen. The wooded hills you gaze out across are especially pretty in autumn, when they turn shades of red and gold.

From the hill, the green trail leads down through meadows, past the site of the early-18th-century homestead of James Allen, and then connects with the blue trail. The blue trail edges into woods that are cool, damp, and shady. Although oaks are still dominant, the number of beech trees begins to increase as the moss-covered trail follows alongside the winding Mill Brook. When you reach the end of the loop, identified by marker #32, turn right on the short blue trail spur that leads back to the parking lot.

Long Point Wildlife Refuge

A trail offering good birding opportunities and lovely pond and ocean views

Hiking distance: 2 miles
Hiking time: 1½ hours

Long Point Wildlife Refuge, on a glacial outwash plain on the south shore of Martha's Vineyard, provides habitat for many species of waterfowl and shorebirds. The 586-acre refuge includes a half mile of South Beach, a white-sand beach popular with both island residents and summer visitors.

The refuge also borders Tisbury Great Pond, Middle Point Cove, and Long Cove, the latter extending more than a mile along the eastern portion of the refuge. The property is a holding of the Massachusetts-based Trustees of Reservations, the oldest private land trust in the country.

The refuge offers a wonderful variety of scenic water views and good bird-watching opportunities. Red-tailed hawks, northern harriers, and rough-legged hawks can sometimes be spotted hunting for mice in the refuge's open meadows. At night, barn owls and screech owls hunt the same fields. Several pairs of ospreys—raptors that prey solely on fish—nest at the refuge in the summer.

Swimming, surf fishing, and picnicking are permitted at the refuge, but there are no rest rooms, beach facilities, or picnic tables.

Access

Access to the refuge differs in summer and winter. In summer, the entrance is at the east side of the property, where you pay to park and

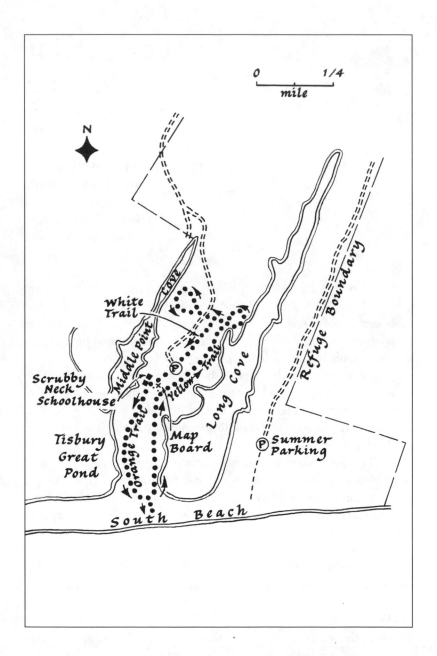

then walk down the beach to reach the nature trails. In winter, parking is near the trailhead.

From mid-June to mid-September, if coming from Edgartown, take West Tisbury Road, and, after passing the entrance road to Martha's Vineyard Airport, continue for 0.3 mile and turn left on Waldon's Bottom Road. From there, it's 2.7 miles to the parking area. Admission is $7 per car, plus $3 for each person age 18 and older. (If you arrive by bicycle or on foot, it's $3 each.) The lot opens at 9 AM daily and, on sunny weekends, often fills up early. No vehicles are admitted after 5 PM.

From mid-September to mid-June, if coming from Edgartown on West Tisbury Road, pass the entrance road to the airport. From there, continue 1.1 miles and turn left onto Deep Bottom Road, a dirt road at a split-rail fence. Bear left at two forks, then, 1 mile in from West Tisbury Road, turn right. Follow the signs another 1.5 miles to the refuge parking lot. There is no admission fee at this time of year.

Parking locations are subject to change. For the latest information, call the refuge at 508-693-3678.

Trail

We combine the refuge's two trails, each a mile long and each starting and ending at the winter-access parking area. One hike crosses open fields to South Beach, and the other passes largely through woodlands; both are along level terrain and easy to walk.

Start at the trail mapboard, which is south of the parking area and at the head of an expansive field. From the mapboard, the orange trail splits; take the path that leads straight ahead. In days past, Long Point was one of the best duck-hunting grounds on the Vineyard, and the building you see at the right was a hunting lodge, open only to members of the exclusive Tisbury Pond Club. The small building in back is the former Scrubby Neck Schoolhouse, a one-room schoolhouse abandoned at the turn of the century. The old hunting lodge is now the home of the wildlife refuge's resident manager, and the schoolhouse has become a storage shed.

The trail leads across a field that is a remnant of the sandplain

*This beautiful stretch of beach is a favorite summertime sunbathing spot
for Vineyard residents.*

grasslands that once covered 40 percent of Martha's Vineyard. Today,
these "coastal prairies" are a far rarer type of habitat due in part to reforestation projects and to the control of natural wildfires that his-
torically protected the grasslands from creeping woodland succession.

In addition to coastal grasses and several rare types of plants,
the field supports a hardy heath plant community, with huckleberry,
blueberry, and bayberry bushes. There are several varieties of shadbush, including the endangered Nantucket shadbush, which produces
a profusion of white flowers in spring. The bright yellow blossoms of
seaside goldenrod provide a colorful accent in late summer, and in autumn the field is an expanse of reds, russets, golds, and browns.

The sandplain grassland is a complex ecosystem that is home to
unusual spiders and wasps, numerous moths and butterflies, small red-
bellied snakes, rare tiger beetles, and other tiny creatures. The large
body of water on the right side of the field is the Tisbury Great
Pond, a salt pond with soft-shelled clams and oysters and its own little beach and boat launch.

As you continue along the orange trail, you'll come to a short spur leading down to South Beach across low sand dunes that are thick with salt-spray rose, dusty miller, and healthy stands of American beach grass. This is a beautiful sweep of beach, with soft white sand and pounding surf that breaks right offshore. Sit and enjoy the sights and sounds of the beach before going back up the orange trail for a walk along the west side of Long Cove.

Shortly before reaching the mapboard near the winter parking area, turn right onto the yellow trail, which leads into a native oak-hickory forest. The trail passes through low scrub oaks that rise from head height to about 25 feet as you move away from the open, exposed meadow and deeper into the woods. About 5 minutes down the path, the trail forks; bear to the right toward Long Cove. In places, the trail edges the cove, offering classic water views that are reminiscent of a Currier & Ives painting. Keep an eye out for great blue herons wading in the marsh and black-crowned night herons roosting in the treetops.

As the trail winds in and out from the water's edge, bear right at all forks. Eventually, the yellow trail circles around and heads west, crossing first the white trail and then the main road. A few minutes later, when the yellow trail forks, follow the loop to the right, through oak woods carpeted with silvery-white lichen, down to Middle Point Cove. At this picturesque site, it's not uncommon to spot a pair of white swans gliding by, a fitting finale to this scenic hike.

Follow the yellow trail back across the road, and this time turn right onto the white trail to return to the parking lot.

Felix Neck Wildlife Sanctuary

A wildlife sanctuary with waterfowl ponds and scenic views

Hiking distance: 2¼ miles
Hiking time: 1¼ hours

Felix Neck Wildlife Sanctuary is on a neck of land that juts out into Sengekontacket Pond on the eastern side of Martha's Vineyard. The 350-acre property, a former farmstead, has been a Massachusetts Audubon Society sanctuary since 1969. The land is crossed with a 4-mile network of well-maintained trails that pass through woodlands and skirt marshes, ponds, and open fields. All the sanctuary trails are level and easy to walk.

More than 100 species of birds have been sighted at the sanctuary. Birds that nest here include ring-necked pheasants, red-tailed hawks, kestrels, screech owls, oystercatchers, and numerous ducks and geese. Cardinals, goldfinches, downy woodpeckers, chickadees, nuthatches, juncos, belted kingfishers, and red-winged blackbirds are commonly spotted, as are the wild turkeys that forage in the field next to the visitors center.

In recent years, ospreys have become summer residents of the sanctuary thanks to the installation of tall poles topped by nesting platforms that attract these rare raptors. Ospreys—eaglelike birds with a 5½-foot wingspan, dark upper plumage, and a white belly—suffered a rapid decline in the 1960s as a result of DDT use, which caused the shells of their eggs to weaken and crack prematurely. Since the banning of DDT, the birds have been making a comeback.

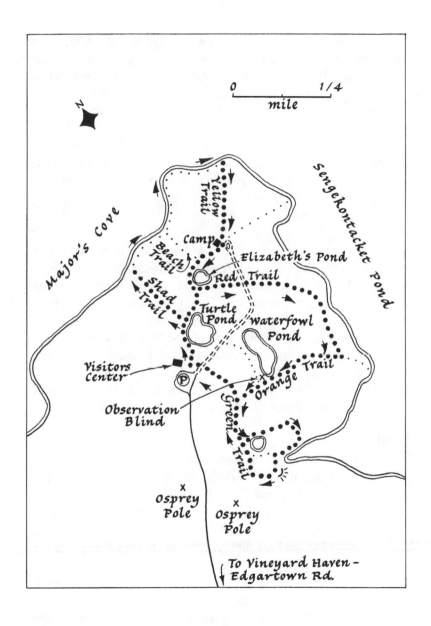

N

0   1/4
mile

Sengekontacket Pond

Major's Cove

Yellow Trail

Camp

Elizabeth's Pond

Beach Trail

Red Trail

Shad Trail

Turtle Pond

Waterfowl Pond

Visitors Center

Orange Trail

Observation Blind

Green Trail

x Osprey Pole

x Osprey Pole

To Vineyard Haven –
Edgartown Rd.

Also known as fish hawks, ospreys survive almost solely on fish and are an impressive bird to watch. While hunting over ponds, they sometimes dive from as high as 175 feet to snatch fish feeding on the surface and on occasion will plunge completely beneath the water.

The sanctuary's visitors center has a display about these birds as well as other natural history exhibits. There's a helpful staff on duty and a gift shop that sells a good collection of nature books and maps. The sanctuary also offers numerous nature programs and a children's summer day camp called Fern and Feather. For more information, call the sanctuary at 508-627-4850.

Access

From its intersection with State Road in Vineyard Haven, take Edgartown Road 4.5 miles south and then turn left at the sanctuary sign. (Alternatively, take Vineyard Haven Road 2 miles north from Oak Bluff Road in Edgartown and turn right.) The sanctuary is 1.5 miles in from the Vineyard Haven–Edgartown Road along a dirt drive.

Admission is free for members of the Massachusetts Audubon Society. For nonmembers, the cost is $3 for adults and $2 for children and senior citizens. The sanctuary trails are open from dawn to 7 PM daily year-round. The visitors center is open from 8 AM to 4 PM daily, except during the off-season, when it is closed on Mondays.

Trail

Start on the yellow trail at the right side of the visitors center. After a couple of minutes through shrubby woodland, the trail leads to a boardwalk along picturesque Turtle Pond. This pond was dug out of the marsh to increase habitat for waterfowl, and the resident mallards find the pond's brackish waters and grassy shoreline ideal for nesting. Look for painted turtles basking in the sun or for big ol' snapping turtles lumbering out onto shore. River otters are sometimes spotted here as well. They move around between the salt marsh and the ponds, leaving footprints and belly-slide marks behind.

From the pond, turn left onto Shad Trail for a short walk through the woods on a springy path cushioned with pads of moss. The trail is named for its shadbush, a slender, gray-barked shrub that

This scenic view is a treat for hikers along the shores of Sengekontacket Pond.

puts on a showy display of white blossoms in spring. Shadbush is also known as Juneberry for its June-ripening fruit that is favored by many birds. The Shad Trail will bring you out to Major's Cove in just a few minutes.

Turn right and begin walking northeast along the shore, which is bordered by a damp marsh with grasses, marsh elder, sea lavender, and stems of succulent glasswort. After a couple of minutes, you'll come to a little sandy beach where the Beach Trail comes in. Don't be surprised to find deer tracks along the shore, for Felix Neck has become a sanctuary for these hoofed creatures as well.

As you continue, the beach becomes marshy again and then rocky. You'll walk over stones mixed with scallop, clam, and broken whelk shells as you round a small point. A few minutes later, as you approach the outermost tip of Felix Neck, look for an opening in the shrubbery on the right, marked with a yellow stake. Climb up the low bank here to connect with the yellow trail.

The yellow trail passes through large pines on the way to an old shingled building, which is used as a nature classroom for the sanctuary's summer camp. Bear right at the "camp" and follow the yellow trail until you're past Elizabeth's Pond, where you turn left onto the red trail. The red trail goes along the south side of this freshwater pond and crosses an old road before leading through woods of oaks and pines and emerging into clearings that afford views of Sengekontacket Pond.

Turn right on the orange trail for a walk past marshland and through a stand of pines to Waterfowl Pond. After crossing the little boardwalk bridge, turn right to reach a nearby observation blind on the edge of the pond. The blind has two-way glass that allows you to get a close-up view of the ducks in the pond while they remain unaware of your presence.

Interpretive materials about the waterfowl that have been sighted in the pond are posted on the walls. The list includes the American black duck, northern pintail, gadwall, American wigeon, wood duck, blue-winged and green-winged teal, common merganser, hooded merganser, red-breasted merganser, and numerous bay ducks, including buffleheads and redheads.

From the observation blind, continue for about 2 minutes on the orange trail, and then turn left onto the green trail (also called the Jessica Hancock Trail). The wide grassy trail passes open meadows with bluebird boxes (which attract more tree swallows than bluebirds), feathery grass, bittersweet, and poison ivy.

In a few minutes, where the trail forks, turn left. You'll pass an inconspicuous little kettle pond on the right, the only naturally occurring pond on Felix Neck. The trail then loops through a woods of maples, oaks, and ferns.

When the trail connects with another loop of the green trail at a wide Y, turn left. In 2 minutes you'll come to the head of a cove on Sengekontacket Pond, one of the most scenic viewpoints in the sanctuary. There's a cattail marsh along the shore and a clear view across the pond to Anthier's Bridge on Beach Road. The distant bridge crosses one of two inlets that cut across an otherwise continuous strip of sandy beach separating Sengekontacket Pond from Nantucket Sound. Although the currents are usually strong enough to keep the inlets clear, they are occasionally dredged to ensure that enough salt water enters the pond for shellfish beds to prosper. Sengekontacket is an Indian word meaning "salty waters."

Sarson's Island, halfway to the bridge, is a nesting site for common terns and is part of the sanctuary property.

Continue along the green trail until you get back to the orange trail, where you turn left for the short walk back to the visitors center.

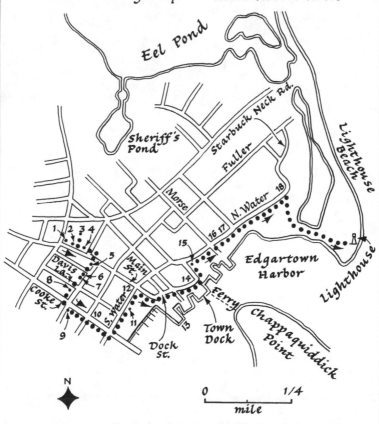

Edgartown

A walking tour through the historic whaling port of Edgartown

Hiking distance: 1½ miles one way
Hiking time: 2–3 hours one way

Edgartown was the site of Martha's Vineyard's first colonial settlement, dating back to 1642, but it was the lucrative 19th-century whaling industry that did the most to shape the town. During the peak whaling years, Edgartown was home to more than a hundred sea captains, men who not only set sail from Edgartown Harbor but who also captained whalers out of Nantucket and New Bedford. No matter where they sailed from, the whaling masters brought their fortunes home to Edgartown, where they retired and built elegant homes.

The houses of these former sea captains still line the brick sidewalks of the central streets, giving the Edgartown of today much the same appearance it had 150 years ago. Not all is the same, of course: The cobblestone streets have been paved over, many of the mansions have become summer homes for wealthy off-islanders, and the harbor that once outfitted whalers is now thick with yachts. Nevertheless, Edgartown remains a well-preserved, historic New England town and an intriguing place to stroll.

Access

Edgartown is on the east side of Martha's Vineyard, 7 miles from Oak Bluffs. There is streetside parking on Main Street; however, in the summer, when Edgartown's narrow streets are congested, visitors should consider taking the summer shuttle that runs from Ocean Park in Oak Bluffs to the corner of Church and Main Streets in Edgartown, near the start of this walk.

Trail

We begin the walk at the corner of Main Street and Planting Field Way. The first house on the left, 105 Main Street, was the home of Captain Thomas Mellen. In the fall of 1871, in an incident that marked the end of the Pacific whaling era, an early Arctic storm trapped 31 whalers and a thousand men in ice floes above the Bering Strait, grinding the ships to pieces. Mellen, captaining the *Europa,* rescued nearly 250 of the trapped sailors.

The stately house next door, which combines elements of Federal and Greek Revival architecture, is the Dr. Daniel Fisher House, built in 1840 for one of Edgartown's most prestigious citizens. Although Dr. Fisher did practice medicine, he made his fortune in whaling, as the owner of a whale oil refinery, in his spermaceti candle factory, and as the founder of the island's first bank.

Behind the Fisher House sits the Vincent House, one of the oldest homes on the island. Surrounded by fruit trees, it looks as if it's been on this site since its construction in the 1670s, but it was actually moved here in 1977 from Mashacket Cove, 2 miles away. The Vincent House is a full cape, with wide, white pine floorboards (called bayboards, for the wood was shipped over from Cape Cod) and a big central brick chimney that supports three fireplaces. From spring to fall, the home is open to the public for a small admission fee.

The grand Greek Revival building on the corner of Main and Church Streets is the Old Whaling Church, built with whaling money in 1843 when most of the island's wealthiest families could be counted in the congregation. This former Methodist church boasts six massive columns, a 92-foot tower with clock and bell, and 50-foot, hand-hewn red pine beams that are joined solely with wooden pegs. It is now a community performing arts center. The Old Whaling Church, Vincent House, and Dr. Daniel Fisher House are all properties of the Martha's Vineyard Historical Preservation Trust.

Turn right onto School Street, at the attractive blue and white St. Elizabeth's Catholic Church, built in the 1920s. The first house after the church, on the right, was built in 1730, though most of the other homes on this street were built in the 1820s.

The Dr. Daniel Fisher House, built in 1840, combines elements of Federal and Greek Revival architecture.

The next house, with the pillared facade, is a former Baptist church built in 1839, which was converted to a Masonic Temple in the early 1900s and more recently into a private residence. The home on the corner of School Street and Davis Lane is the former Thaxter Academy, built as a private school in 1825. It is noteworthy for its decorative doorway.

Next up is the engrossing Martha's Vineyard Historical Society complex, on the corner of School and Cooke Streets. The society's main museum contains whaling-era paraphernalia, scrimshaw, ship logs, and period photos, including the stoic portraits of 110 Edgartown whaling masters. The Carriage Shed out back houses a beautifully restored 1852 fire engine, a whaleboat, harpoons, and blubber hooks. In summer, guided tours are given of the Thomas Cooke House, a 12-room Colonial home built in 1765. Also on the grounds is a magnificent Fresnel lens, consisting of 1,009 crystal prisms, which cast its beam from the Gay Head Light for nearly a century before being replaced by an electric beacon. An admission fee is charged to tour the complex.

Continue the walk by going east on Cooke Street, past the old Federated Church, and left on South Water Street. The Coffin family at one time owned much of this area, and most of the houses along this street that weren't lived in by Coffins were built by them. Jared Coffin and Thomas Coffin were two of the most respected carpenters of the day, and the houses they built invariably reflect skilled craftsmanship.

A block down South Water Street, on the right, is a big pagoda tree, said to be the largest in North America. The tree was brought from China as a sapling in 1837 by Captain Thomas Milton, who built the adjacent house at 9 South Water Street three years later for the extravagant sum of $900.

At the corner, marked by Edgartown National Bank, turn right and walk down toward the water. The weathered, shingled building out on the wharf is the elite Edgartown Yacht Club, which counts a number of celebrities, including Walter Cronkite, among its members. Follow Dock Street to the left along the harbor and you'll soon come to Town Dock, where the *On Time Ferry* plies the waters to Chappaquiddick, carrying just three cars at a time for the short hop across the harbor. Be sure to climb the two-story viewing platform next to the dock, which offers a panoramic view of Edgartown Harbor.

Across from the ferry terminal is Old Sculpin Gallery, a summertime art gallery that was once the workshop of craftsman Manuel Swartz Roberts. Roberts built catboats and other craft of such high caliber that two of his boats are on display in the Smithsonian. The yard beside the gallery, where a big anchor lies, was the site of Dr. Daniel Fisher's whale oil refinery.

From the dock, turn left up Daggett Street and then right onto North Water Street, which is lined with the stately homes of former sea captains. Federal and Greek Revival architecture predominates, but there are also older Colonial homes. One of the finest examples of Colonial architecture is the Daggett Inn, a former sailors' boardinghouse at the corner of Daggett and North Water. The inn was built in 1750 on the site of the Vineyard's first tavern, where in 1660 tavern owner John Daggett was fined 5 shillings for "selling strong liquor" in addition to the permissible ale and beer. Part of the old tavern, including a beehive fireplace, is incorporated into the current dining room on the garden level.

As was the style in the mid-19th century, most of the homes along North Water Street are of white clapboards with black shutters, but each has its own unique features. You'll notice beautifully detailed doorways, fanlights of handblown glass, elaborate porticoes, and other rich ornamentation.

At 86 and 88 North Water Street, you'll find two elegant, Federal-style houses. The three-story Captain Jared Fisher House was built in 1832 by Thomas Coffin. It remained in Captain Fisher's family for five generations until 1961, when it became a property of the Society for the Preservation of New England Antiquities. The house next door was built in an identical style, minus the third story, for Captain Edwin Coffin in 1840. Both houses have widow's walks—railed, rooftop walkways used by sea captains' wives as lookouts from which they watched for their husbands' boats to return from sea.

Continue a block and a half until reaching the Harborview Hotel, a large Victorian hostelry dating to the 1890s. Opposite the hotel, take the path leading across the causeway to the Edgartown

Lighthouse. The original lighthouse, a two-story lightkeeper's house with a tower on the roof, was built in 1828 on an artificial island of cut granite blocks. Over time, sands built up around the island, creating the beach that the current white tower, erected in 1938, sits on today. Lighthouse Beach is a good vantage point for watching yachts cruise in and out of the harbor. A fitting place to end the walk, it's a worthy beach for strolling and, on a warm summer's day, a popular place to sunbathe and swim.

Cape Poge Wildlife Refuge and Wasque Reservation

A long walk along a beautiful sweep of white sand beach backed by low, windswept dunes

Hiking distance: 12 miles
Hiking time: 6–7 hours

Cape Poge Wildlife Refuge and Wasque Reservation are two nature reserves that encompass almost the entire east coast of Chappaquiddick Island. Cape Poge, the larger, consists of 509 acres of undeveloped barrier beach, sand dunes, salt marshes, and salt ponds. With a total of more than 6 miles of beach fronting Nantucket Sound and the shellfish-rich waters of Cape Poge Bay, the refuge provides habitat for thousands of seabirds and shorebirds.

Wasque Reservation, to the south, encompasses 200 acres of heathlands, marshlands, wooded upland, low sand cliffs, brackish ponds, and sandy beaches. It is from Wasque that Chappaquiddick is connected to the rest of Martha's Vineyard via a stretch of barrier beach that runs along the south side of Katama Bay. This barrier beach has broken open at least nine times in the past two hundred years, the latest in 1976. When the breaks occur, the southern end of Katama Bay opens to the Atlantic and Chappaquiddick becomes a true island. Wasque is an Indian name that means "the ending."

This hike starts at Wasque Reservation, at the southeastern tip of Chappaquiddick, goes up the long, narrow barrier beach of Cape Poge Wildlife Refuge to the lighthouse at the island's northern point,

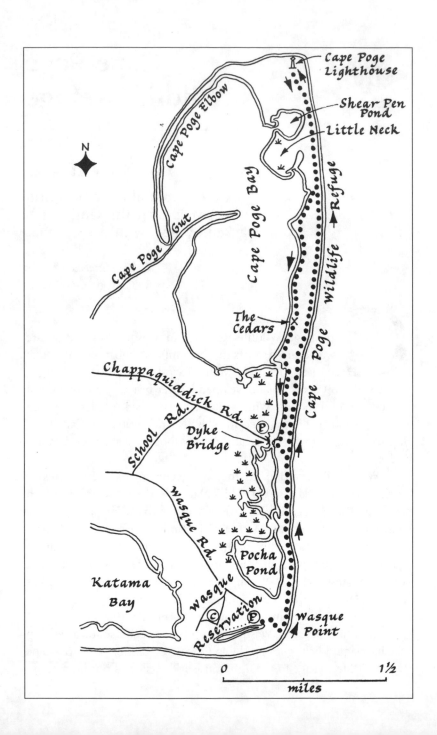

and then comes back again. The full trek should be attempted only by those in good shape. It's not only long but also strenuous, because much of it is across soft sand that can make sections of the walk seem more like a trudge than a hike. It's unshaded—hot in summer and cold in winter—so dress accordingly and take plenty of water. Still, the lonely, windswept beauty of the beach and the wild open ocean are ample reward.

Cape Poge and Wasque are both managed by the Trustees of Reservations, a nonprofit land trust dedicated to preserving properties of exceptional scenic, historic, and ecological value.

Wampanoag Indians once made their summer home at Wasque, close to the shores of Katama Bay. In the 1640s, Thomas Mayhew, who established the first British colony on the Vineyard, bought the land at the northern end of Cape Poge Bay, from Little Neck to the end of the Cape Poge Elbow. In the latter half of the 1600s, colonists began to bring their sheep and cattle to Wasque and Cape Poge to winter on salt-marsh hay, but they did not settle the area.

In 1802, as Edgartown was beginning to develop into one of the world's chief whaling ports, a lighthouse was built on the northern tip of Cape Poge to help guide whalers around the point. The lighthouse caretaker and his family were the first year-round white settlers on Chappaquiddick. In the mid-1850s, during the height of the whaling era, the lighthouse guided more than ten thousand ships a year into Edgartown Harbor.

Cape Poge also played a minor role during World War II, when the U.S. military stationed about three dozen soldiers on the beach to watch for German submarines. Not a single enemy vessel was ever spotted, and it surely must rank as one of the most peaceful places to have been stationed during wartime.

Whereas Cape Poge was protected from settlement by its remoteness, Wasque, on the other hand, was settled by a succession of fishermen, farmers, and sailors. During the hustle and bustle of the whaling era, most of Chappaquiddick was, for all practical purposes, a suburb of Edgartown, thick with sailors and sea captains. By the end of the 19th century, Wasque had become a popular summer beach resort.

Today, Wasque Reservation and Cape Poge Wildlife Refuge provide habitat for red-tailed hawks, harriers, kestrels, short-eared owls,
nesting ospreys, sandpipers, piping plovers, oystercatchers, snowy
egrets, green herons, black-crowned night herons, and great blue
herons, as well as migrating waterfowl and the ubiquitous herring and
black-backed gulls.

The sandy dunes are also an important nesting site for least
terns, who gather in colonies to afford their eggs and young some
protection from predators such as hawks, gulls, skunks, and raccoons.
The terns have an excellent defense against human invaders as well—
loud cries and aggressive dive-bombing attacks—as you'll readily find
out should you chance too close to their nesting sites!

Hiking, surf fishing, swimming, and picnicking are allowed on
the properties, though the only facilities are summertime rest rooms
and picnic tables at Wasque.

Access

The *On Time Ferry* makes the 5-minute run from Edgartown's Town
Dock to Chappaquiddick Island at frequent intervals daily. The ferry
runs from 7 AM to midnight from June to mid-October, with somewhat reduced hours the rest of the year. For ferry information, call
508-627-9794.

Once on the island, take Chappaquiddick Road away from the
dock for 2.5 miles and, at the bend, curve right onto School Road.
After 0.8 mile, turn left onto Wasque Road and take it 1.2 miles to
Wasque Reservation. From June 1 to September 30, Wasque Reservation charges an admission fee of $3 per vehicle plus $3 per adult;
the rest of the year there are no fees.

The Dyke Bridge, which for years was condemned and closed
to the public, has been repaired and once again provides direct access
to the Cape Poge refuge. If you want to approach Cape Poge from
here, it would cut almost 4 miles off the hike. There's a place to park
before the bridge. The aforementioned $3 admission fee applies dur-
ing the summer season; there are no fees the rest of the year.

While the Trustees of Reservations owns most of the property
that the hike covers, there is a 1.5-mile section of the beach near the

Dyke Bridge that is owned by the state, which purchased it from private owners in 1995 to ensure public access. If you have any questions about the reservation, or Trustee-sponsored nature tours, contact the Trustees of Reservations at 508-627-3599.

Wasque and Cape Poge are also open to over-sand vehicles (OSV), so expect to see some traffic along the way. This beach is a popular area for surf fishermen, who drive their OSVs up to the northern part of Cape Poge to cast for migrating bluefish and striped bass.

Trail

This hike takes in all of Chappaquiddick's east side. Although it's largely a beach walk, you'll also pass salt ponds, estuaries, heathlands, salt marshes, and red cedar thickets.

Begin the hike at Wasque Reservation by taking the long boardwalk that leads to the beach from the parking area. Then head north along the shore to start the walk up to the lighthouse, 6 miles away.

To your right will be the open Atlantic, and on your left, Pocha Pond, a picturesque, brackish pond surrounded by marsh grasses. Pocha Pond, which is connected by a lagoon to Cape Poge Bay, is the breeding ground for many of the scallops that flourish in the bay. After about 1¼ miles up the beach, you'll come to the point where Pocha Pond narrows into the lagoon and is crossed by the Dyke Bridge.

The beach north from the Dyke Bridge is a good place to identify shells. We've found numerous large whelks, both the channeled and knobbed types, as well as moon shells, blue mussels, Atlantic ribbed mussels, sand dollars, common Atlantic slipper shells, the delicate eastern white slipper, jingle shells, chestnut astartes, oysters, clams, and scallops.

A little over a mile north of Dyke Bridge, you'll come to The Cedars, the name given to the long strip of red cedar trees that stand inland of the dunes. Gnarled and bent by the strong winds that sweep across the sandbar, these mature trees are so stunted that most are only 5 or 6 feet high. Still, they rise above the surrounding vegetation as a little oasis of greenery in sharp contrast to the beige dunes, creating one of the more unusual sights along this trail.

The boardwalk at Wasque Reservation leads out to the beach.

The dunes themselves are far from barren. Not only do they have a sparse covering of beach grass, but the top of the dunes provides a foothold for clusters of seaside goldenrod, bayberry, and salt-spray rose. The last, *Rosa rugosa,* has magenta or white flowers with a sweet perfume and blooms well into late fall.

In the summer, boardwalks are laid down in a couple of places across the primary dunes that separate the OSV trails from the beach, and you can cross back and forth. During the off-season, however, the boardwalks are taken up to prevent them from being buried by sand swept inland during winter storms. Where there are no boardwalks, hikers are asked to avoid crossing or walking on the face of the dunes and to stay at least 10 feet away from the beach grass, whose shallow, wide-spreading root system helps stabilize the dunes. Beach grass may look hardy, but once a shoot is broken, it cannot regenerate and will die.

Erosion can be a serious problem, and not only for the native dune ecosystem. The original Cape Poge lighthouse, built in 1802, survived only 41 years of winter storms before the bluff it stood on was claimed by the sea. The lighthouse built to replace it suffered a similar fate.

In the early 1960s, the current lighthouse, a 40-foot, white-shingled tower built in 1893, sat back 150 feet from the shoreline. By the mid-1980s, the crumbling bluff had closed the gap to about 20 feet, and the 4 acres that once made up the Coast Guard station had nearly all washed into the sea.

In 1987, after the Coast Guard had negotiated a lease on new land with the Trustees of Reservations, a "sky crane" helicopter picked up the lighthouse and moved it 500 feet inland. No doubt, in time the shifting sands will catch up with it once again!

Approximately ⅓ mile before reaching the lighthouse, you'll come to an OSV road leading off the beach. Turn inland onto the road and follow it up to the lighthouse. Cape Poge's last lighthouse keeper was replaced by an automatic electric light in 1964. The area does support a population of white-tailed deer, however, and if you approach the lighthouse quietly, there's a fair chance you'll spot them.

On the return walk from the lighthouse, you can either retrace your steps along the beach or take the inland OSV trails that offer lovely views of Cape Poge Bay and Pocha Pond. During the fall season, you're likely to spot many small boats scalloping in Cape Poge Bay. The richest bay scallop grounds on the East Coast, Cape Poge produces 50 percent of the state's harvest.

Nantucket

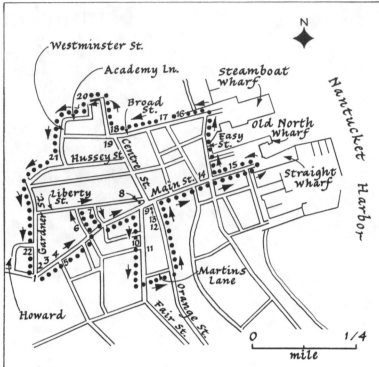

Westminster St.

Academy Ln.

steamboat wharf

N

Nantucket Harbor

Broad St.

17 16

Old North Wharf

18

Easy St.

19 Centre St.

Hussey St.

21

15

Straight wharf

Liberty St.

8

Main St. 14

Gardner St.

7

6

9 13

12

10

11

22 Gardner St.

3 4

2 5

1

Martins Lane

Fair St.

Orange St.

Howard

0   1/4
mile

KEY

1. Civil War Monument
2. 105 Main Street
3. Thomas Macy House
4. Three Bricks
5. William Hadwen House
6. Coffin School
7. Nathaniel Macy House
8. Pacific National Bank
9. Murray's Toggery Shop
10. Quaker Meetinghouse and Fair Street Museum
11. St. Paul's Episcopal Church
12. Unitarian Church
13. Philip Folger House
14. Pacific Club
15. Thomas Macy Warehouse
16. Whaling Museum
17. Peter Foulger Museum
18. Jared Coffin House
19. Captain Pollard House
20. Old North Church
21. Timothy Barnard House
22. Fire Hose Cart House

Nantucket Town

A walking tour through the historic town of Nantucket

Hiking distance: 2 miles
Hiking time: 2–4 hours, depending
on time spent at historic sites

The town of Nantucket is a charmingly preserved early New England seaport. Once the center of the world's whaling industry, Nantucket's rich history is reflected in the hundreds of 18th- and 19th-century homes that still line the town's cobblestone streets—the highest concentration of such period houses anywhere in the country.

Nantucket was an isolated community of farmers and sheep herders until 1712, when islanders, who had been hunting right whales that swam close to shore, were blown off course into deeper waters, where they harpooned their first sperm whale. So impressed were they with the superior quality of the oil that the catch spurred the beginning of a new industry—deep-sea whaling. The hunt eventually led hundreds of Nantucket whalers far into the Pacific, where sperm whales were most plentiful. In the early 19th century, Nantucket boasted an all-time high of nearly eight thousand inhabitants, almost all of them involved with whaling in one way or another. Mansions built by rich whale oil merchants and the homes of whaling captains filled the town. The discovery of petroleum spelled the end of the whaling era, and by the 1870s, resource-poor Nantucket was largely impoverished, with a lot of grand houses but a population of just two thousand.

At the turn of the 20th century, visitors from New York and Boston discovered that Nantucket made a fine place to summer, and tourism has been a mainstay of the economy ever since. Many of the larger old houses have been turned into inns or second homes for wealthy families. The Nantucket Historical Association maintains 10 historic sites that are open to the public: the Whaling Museum and the Peter Foulger Museum year-round, the others during the tourist season and holiday periods. At this writing, a visitors pass to all the historical association sites costs $10 for adults, $5 for children under 15.

Access

The Steamship Authority runs ferries from Hyannis to Nantucket year-round, docking near the center of town at the intersection of Easy and Broad Streets. In summer, Hy-Line Cruises runs ferries from Hyannis and Martha's Vineyard to Nantucket, landing at Straight Dock at the end of Lower Main Street. For information, call the Steamship Authority at 508-477-8600 or Hy-Line Cruises at 508-778-2600.

Trail

We begin this walking tour at the intersection of Gardner and Main Streets, which is marked by a Civil War monument oddly placed in the center of the road and best viewed from the sidewalk. Hundreds of Nantucketers volunteered to fight for the Union cause, influenced in part by the island's prominence in the abolitionist movement. It was on Nantucket that escaped slave Frederick Douglass made his debut as an orator in 1841.

From the monument, head east down Main Street. The first house on the left, at 105 Main Street, is one of the oldest in town, dating back to 1690. The eastern part of the house was moved from Sherburne, the island's original colonial settlement 2 miles west of here. In 1700, a fierce winter storm closed off Sherburne's harbor (now Capaum Pond); consequently, the settlement shifted to the present-day town of Nantucket.

The next place of interest is the Thomas Macy House, 99 Main Street, which was once the home of a prominent shipowner and is known for its decorative doorway.

Following this house are the "Three Bricks," three identical

Georgian brick mansions built in the 1830s by whale oil merchant Joseph Starbuck for his three sons, George, Matthew, and William. Starbuck, who owned 23 whaling ships, presented the keys upon completion but retained the property titles for more than a decade, until his sons were full partners in his business. Notice the horse hitching post, one of many that can still be found on sidewalks around town.

Across the street are two stately, white Greek Revival mansions with high porticoes. Built in the 1840s by "oil man" William Hadwen, they reflect the prosperity and elegance at the height of the whaling era. Hadwen built the home on the corner for himself and the other for his niece. Hadwen's mansion now belongs to the Nantucket Historical Association and is open to visitors during the season.

As you continue down Main Street, you'll notice a prominent feature of 19th-century Nantucket houses: friendship steps, a double set of steps leading to the front door that allowed hosts to greet guests from either direction.

When you reach Winter Street, turn left. You'll soon come to the Coffin School, a Greek Revival brick structure with Doric columns that was erected as a private school in 1852 and is now used as a community center.

Turn right at the next corner, onto Liberty Street. The weathered, saltbox-style house with the central fireplace on the corner of Liberty and Walnut Lane is the Nathaniel Macy House, built in Sherburne in 1723 before being moved to its present location.

Take Walnut Lane back to Main Street and turn left, continuing to the intersection of Main and Fair Streets. On the left is the Pacific National Bank (circa 1818), with a name that attests to the far-flung influence of Nantucket's whaling days. It was from an observatory on the bank's rooftop in 1847 that Maria Mitchell discovered a new comet, launching her career in astronomy. Opposite the bank is Murray's Toggery Shop, where Nantucket native R.H. Macy opened his first store before heading off to New York and establishing the now-famous Macy's department store.

Turn right on Fair Street, and, a block down, you'll come to the Quaker Meetinghouse. Quakers came to Nantucket in the early

1700s to escape religious persecution and soon became an important influence on the island's social and economic life. This structure was built as a school in 1838, at a time when nearly half of the islanders were Quaker, and was later used as a prayer house, a function it still serves each Sunday in summer. The attached Fair Street Museum features changing art exhibits. Both are owned by the Nantucket Historical Association.

A short way down Fair Street on the left is St. Paul's Episcopal Church, an attractive granite church with Tiffany windows, built in 1901.

Continue down Fair Street, turn left on Martins Lane, then turn left again on Orange Street, another street thick with the former homes of sea captains. On the left side of Orange Street, before reaching the Unitarian Church, is Nantucket's one and only experiment with town houses, a five-plex built in 1831 by speculators out to test the waters. Although the Federal-style building is appealing enough, the concept never gained popularity.

The glowing gold dome of the Unitarian Church is one of the most prominent sites in the village and has long been a landmark for those arriving by boat. Built in 1809, its 109-foot wooden clock tower served as the site of the town's fire watch in earlier times. The tower bell, brought from Lisbon in 1815, has a melodious tone and still tolls at 7 AM, noon, and 9 PM daily.

Continue down Orange Street until you reach the commercial end of Main Street, which has changed little in appearance since the late 19th century. Its cobbled streets are still lit by old-fashioned gas lights, and its brick sidewalks are lined with benches under stately elm trees; the old pharmacy even has a soda jerk serving ice cream and sandwiches. In front of the circa-1831 Philip Folger House, look for a white marble slab embedded in the sidewalk that marks the bounds of the Great Fire of 1846. The fire began in a hat shop on the corner of Union and Main Streets, and within hours it had destroyed one-third of the town, including nearly the entire business district clear down to the docks.

Walk down Main Street to the Pacific Club, a three-story brick building constructed in 1772 by shipowner William Rotch. It was

*These three brick mansions were built in the 1830s by whale oil merchant
Joseph Starbuck for his three sons.*

Rotch's vessels, the *Beaver* and the *Dartmouth,* that carried the English
tea dumped overboard in Boston Harbor during the Boston Tea Party.
The *Beaver* went on to become the first whaler to round Cape Horn.
In 1789, the building here became the site of one of the first U.S.
Customs Service houses, indicative of Nantucket's importance as a
trading center. In the mid-1800s, it housed a club whose membership
was limited to captains of the Pacific whaling fleet.

From the Pacific Club, the road continues as Lower Main Street.
The brick building across from the A&P is the Thomas Macy Warehouse, built in 1846 to outfit whalers.

Continue for a stroll down picturesque Straight Wharf. Built in
1723 to serve whalers, it was the town's first wharf and today is lined
with fishing boats, both commercial and charter. When you return
from the wharf, turn right on Easy Street. You'll soon pass Old North
Wharf, where shingled cottages sit on pilings above the water, with
rowboats tied to their back porches.

At the end of Easy Street, where the Steamboat Authority ships dock, turn left onto Broad Street. At the next corner is the Whaling Museum, which displays an extensive collection of scrimshaw, harpoons, and other whaling paraphernalia, as well as the skeleton of a 43-foot finback whale. The museum building was constructed in 1846 as a factory to refine whale oil for lamp fuel and to make spermaceti candles. Next door, the Peter Foulger Museum has an eclectic assortment of Nantucket memorabilia donated from private collections. Peter Foulger, a prominent early settler who served as an interpreter for the Indians, was the grandfather of Benjamin Franklin. Other descendants of his include astronomer Maria Mitchell, social reformer Lucretia Mott, and coffee empire founder James Folger, all born on Nantucket.

The walk continues up Broad Street, passing a couple of attractive Victorian homes that have been turned into inns. Nantucket was in the throes of a post-whaling depression during the years when Victorian architecture was in vogue in the rest of the nation, and there are few such buildings in town.

When you reach Centre Street, pause for a moment. The three-story brick building on the right is the Jared Coffin House, one of the town's most fashionable inns. The building diagonally opposite, now a gift shop, was once the home of George Pollard Jr., captain of the whaler *Essex,* which was sunk in the Pacific in 1819 after being twice rammed head-on by a charging 85-foot sperm whale. Only Captain Pollard and 4 of his 19-man crew survived, after having drifted for three months and resorting to cannibalism of their fellow crew members to stay alive. Their ordeal, which was recorded by first mate Owen Chase, became the inspiration for Herman Melville's *Moby-Dick.*

Turn right on Centre Street, and you'll soon reach the steps to the Old North Church. The church, built in 1834, has a trompe l'oeil painting behind the altar and a huge chandelier. In summer, for a nominal fee, you can climb the tower, which offers Nantucket's most panoramic view.

Rather than return to Centre Street, walk south from the church and take the first right, down Academy Lane. About 300 feet down, take the next left onto unmarked Westminster Street, which you follow to its end at Hussey Street, where you turn right. At the corner of Hussey and Westminster Streets is the Timothy Barnard House, one of the neighborhood's oldest homes, a 2½-story, shingled lean-to built in 1758.

Follow Hussey Street to its end, turn left, and continue down Gardner Street until reaching the Fire Hose Cart House on the corner of Gardner and Howard Streets. Built in 1886, it is the last of the neighborhood firehouses that were once located throughout the town. The building contains an antique fire cart and is open and free during the season. Follow Gardner Street back to the Civil War monument, where this walking tour ends.

Long Pond
Public Sanctuary
A short walk along a picturesque pond near Madaket village

Hiking distance: 1¼ mile
Hiking time: 45 minutes

Long Pond is a long and narrow waterway that cuts across nearly the entire island of Nantucket from north to south. It originated as a glacial meltwater stream flowing across Nantucket's outwash plains, but over time a narrow buffer of sand developed along the ocean at the stream's south end, turning it into a pond.

The trail through Long Pond Public Sanctuary begins along the shores of Long Pond, skirts a bog, and then makes a loop through an unspoiled heathland. This strikingly scenic area is a rich habitat for wildlife, including great blue herons and white-tailed deer.

The 64-acre property is a holding of the Nantucket Land Bank, which was created in 1984 to acquire and manage lands that are deemed important to the preservation and recreational needs of Nantucket. Funds for land acquisition are generated from a 2 percent transfer fee levied against real estate transactions on Nantucket. The land bank preserves scenic landscapes, protects rare species habitat, and provides public access to open space. Its properties are marked by boundary posts with the land bank's green-and-white-striped logo.

Access

From the town of Nantucket, take either Cliff Road or Madaket Road west. The two roads intersect at Swain Hill, from where you continue 2.9 miles west on Madaket Road. Then, just before entering the village of Madaket, turn left on Cambridge Avenue at the TRIS-TRAM'S LANDING sign. Follow Cambridge Avenue 0.3 mile until it

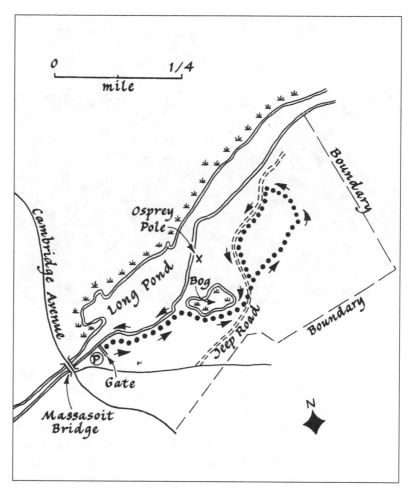

crosses Massasoit Bridge, and then immediately turn left into the sanctuary's grassy parking area, which is marked with a boundary post and sign.

Trail

The trail begins at a large wooden gate at the edge of the parking area and runs northeast on a grassy path fronting Long Pond. From here, the narrow, bending waterway looks more like a river than a pond, except that the waters are still. It's a lovely, peaceful scene.

This grassy trail runs along the side of Long Pond, where great blue herons can sometimes be seen.

The cattails and the tall, feathery grasses that line the shoreline provide a screen for great blue herons, which feed at the water's edge. Cattails start off in the spring with double heads of flowers, the male flowers encircling directly above the tight cylinder of female flowers. After giving off their pollen, the male flowers fall off, leaving a bare spike tip above the velvety brown female section. The cattail was an important food source for American Indians, who ate the tender shoots and ground the rootstock into meal.

As you continue walking along the pond, you'll see a tall post that has been erected near the shoreline in an effort to attract a pair of nesting ospreys.

After about 5 minutes, the trail turns inland from the pond and begins to skirt a bog. In the soft soil on this part of the trail, it's common to find the hoofprints of white-tailed deer, which feed upon the grasses and shrubs growing in the sanctuary. Because deer have a keen sense of smell and are largely nocturnal, seeing them is far less common than seeing their tracks. If you make this hike in the early morning or at dusk, however, there's a chance you'll hear a whistling snort off in the thickets, a clear sign that deer have spotted you.

After a few minutes of walking, you'll reach a grassy jeep road. Turn left onto the road and walk for about a minute until you come to a clearing cut through arrowwood and bayberry scrub on the right side of the road. Turn right here, where the trail continues as a wide swath up across sandplain grasslands, an ecosystem that is far more complex than it appears. In addition to the common heathland plants, such as bayberry and bearberry, the sandy, acidic soil harbors lesser-known plants and rare wildflowers. The trail loops back to the jeep road, where you'll then turn left.

As you walk back, you'll see a bit more of Long Pond and pass closer to the osprey pole, now on the right side of the trail. While walking along the jeep road, look for the unusual earth star, a tough mushroom with a puffball center. In wet weather, its leathery outer coat unfolds much like the petals of a flower, absorbing water from the ground. When the air is dry, the petals curl up around the puffball, holding in thousands of spores until the plant eventually releases them to the wind. The open earth star is about 2½ inches across.

When you reach the footpath where you first turned onto the jeep road, turn right and follow the trail to the trailhead back the way you came.

34

The Sanford Farm, Ram Pasture and The Woods

A long walk through a diverse conservation area offering pond, marsh, and ocean views

Hiking distance: 6½ miles
Hiking time: 3½ hours

This walk, which begins in the Sanford Farm property and continues through the adjacent Ram Pasture and The Woods, is the top hiking destination on Nantucket. The lower 634 acres that comprise Ram Pasture and The Woods were purchased by the Nantucket Conservation Foundation in 1971 to protect them from impending development, while the 300-acre Sanford Farm became conservation lands in the mid-1980s.

The properties are important both for their historical significance and for the diverse natural environments they encompass. The Sanford Farm area, along with the land running north to the sea, was the site of Nantucket's original colonial settlement, while vast tracts of Ram Pasture and The Woods were set aside by the colonists as grazing land. The properties, which include open moors, woods, marshes, freshwater ponds, and ocean beach, now provide a protected habitat for rare plants and birds. A series of interpretive plaques placed along the trail offer insight into the history, geology, and flora and fauna of the area.

The trail is marked and well maintained, and it's an easy walk with just a few low hills. We walk the entire trail network, a hike that travels all the way to the ocean and back, taking in two loop trails en route. It's possible, however, to shorten the hike by doing only the

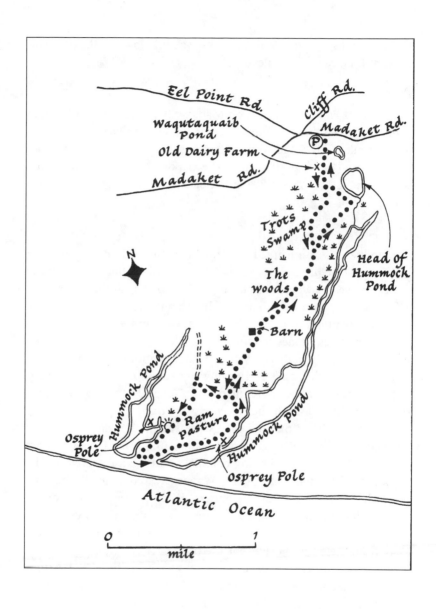

Eel Point Rd.

Cliff Rd.

Waqutaquaib Pond

Madaket Rd.

Old Dairy Farm

Madaket Rd.

Trots Swamp

Head of Hummock Pond

The woods

Barn

Hummock Pond

Ram Pasture

Hummock Pond

Osprey Pole

Osprey Pole

N

Atlantic Ocean

0   1

mile

first loop, a distance of 1¾ miles, or by walking down to the barn and back, a distance of 3¼ miles.

Access

The Sanford Farm trailhead is on Madaket Road, about 2 miles from Nantucket town. From the town center, either head west on Madaket Road or take Cliff Road west to its intersection with Madaket Road, turn left, and continue 0.2 mile. The parking area is clearly posted with a NANTUCKET CONSERVATION FOUNDATION sign and a boundary marker.

Trail

The trailhead is at a marked turnstile at the left side of the parking lot. The hike begins along an old dirt road, which after a few minutes passes an overgrown cellar hole and collapsed silo, all that remains of a former dairy farm that operated here until the Great Depression. The trail continues through a field of grasses and wildflowers, then, in a few minutes, comes to a fork. Ignore the path to the left, which loops off the main trail, and continue straight ahead. You'll go up and down some gentle slopes and through mixed brushland before edging Trots Swamp, a freshwater marsh. In August, keep an eye open for the fruiting highbush blueberries along the trail.

Not long after the trail leaves the swamp, it's flanked by two wooden posts where a gate once marked the boundary into Ram Pasture and The Woods. During colonial times, Ram Pasture and The Woods, then known as the Long Woods, was communally held by Nantucket's original European settlers. Each of the 27 freeholders had the right to fatten 20 sheep on the property. At the lower end of Long Woods, they established a separate area for rams to keep them away from the ewes and prevent the birth of lambs during the cold winter season. Today, the grassy meadows are a feeding spot for ring-necked pheasants and a hunting ground for hawks and short-eared owls, which prey on meadow voles and deer mice.

After passing the posts, you'll see Hummock Pond off in the distance to the left. In the same direction, you can spot an osprey pole, one of several on the property that have been occupied by nest-

Pine tree in spring

ing ospreys. At a large field, the loop trail merges back in on the left, but continue straight ahead.

After the path enters the woods, look for the tracks of white-tailed deer along the trail and for deer runs leading off through the thickets. The deer are not native to Nantucket but were introduced earlier this century by one of the island's summer residents. Among the varied trees and shrubs found in this area are hawthorn, which has spiky thorns more than an inch long and provides a protective habitat for songbirds, and winterberry, which sports bright red berries long after the fall foliage has dropped. In spring, honeysuckle blooms sweetly, and in late summer, sweet pepperbush releases a spicy fragrance.

After about 20 minutes, the trail leads up to a hilltop barn. From the clearing surrounding the barn, there are expansive views of Hummock Pond to the left, the Atlantic Ocean straight ahead, and distant Madaket to the right. The tall, pink-purple joe-pye weed that blooms in the field in the latter half of summer was named for an Indian medicine man who reportedly used the plant to stem a typhus outbreak in the Bay State.

From the barn, the trail continues down the slope through tall thickets. After about 15 minutes, when a side trail comes in on the left, continue straight ahead. In about 100 yards, you'll come to plaque #19, where the trail veers right to begin the Ram Pasture loop.

After about 10 minutes, take the trail that comes in on the left, which leads across an outwash plain of heaths and grasses, down along the marsh, and out toward the beach. About ½ mile along this trail, you'll come to a lookout offering a clear view of an osprey pole, which has had a pair of nesting ospreys each year since the mid-1980s.

The trail now continues on a neck of land that runs down to the ocean, separating the two sections of Hummock Pond. Formerly a single, U-shaped pond, the "Blizzard of '78" drove piles of sand up into the southern reaches of Hummock Pond, and it has been divided into two bodies of water ever since. A few hundred feet after the trail makes a sharp turn and heads east, there's a step that crosses the trailside fence, allowing access to a white sand beach. The trail then crosses fields that are periodically burned to prevent reforestation, thus maintaining the grasslands. There are fine views of Hummock Pond before the path turns north through thickets of aromatic bayberry and completes the Ram Pasture loop.

Turn right onto the main trail, which is marked by a trail post, and begin the walk back. After about half an hour, you'll reach plaque #7 and the start of the second loop. Turn right to begin the 20-minute loop trail, which passes through some low uplands and offers scenic views of both Hummock Pond and Head of Hummock Pond. The trail enters a grove of pitch pines just before merging back to the main trail, where you turn right for the short walk back to the parking lot.

Windswept
Cranberry Bog
A walk through working cranberry bogs to a scenic pond

Hiking distance: 1½ miles
Hiking time: 1 hour

Windswept Cranberry Bog contains 230 acres of working cranberry bogs surrounded by marshes, ponds, and woodlands. The property is a holding of the Nantucket Conservation Foundation, a member-supported, non-profit corporation that preserves open space and places of unusual natural and historic significance on Nantucket. The foundation's success in acquiring environmentally sensitive properties is unparalleled. Since its founding in 1963, the corporation has acquired almost two hundred properties, which collectively represent more than 25 percent of the land on Nantucket. The Nantucket Conservation Foundation welcomes visitors to explore its diverse properties, which include beaches, moors, meadows, and forests, as well as cranberry bogs, both wild and cultivated.

The cranberry is one of only a handful of edible fruits native to North America. American Indians called it "bitter berry" and ate it sweetened with maple sap. They also mixed cranberries with deer meat and fat and dried it into flat cakes called pemmican, a staple food that helped carry them through the winter. The Indians introduced the vitamin C–rich cranberries to early settlers, and when Nantucket whalers left port for distant seas, they packed a full store of the hardy berries to prevent scurvy.

Following the demise of whaling, Nantucketers, looking for another way to make a living, began growing cranberries on a commercial scale. By the early 20th century, the island could boast of having the world's largest contiguous cranberry bog.

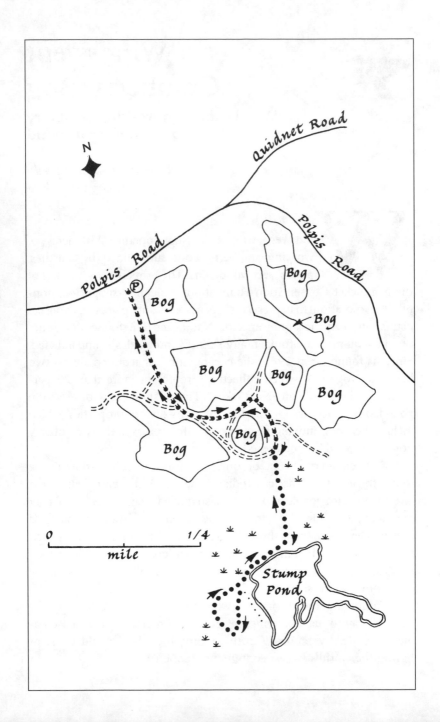

Cranberries, like other members of the heath family, thrive in sandy, acidic soils. A low, evergreen vine, the plant grows best in moist places where the water table is about a foot below the surface. In early summer, the plants produce pinkish white flowers that, with a little imagination, look like the beak and head of a crane. Because of this resemblance, early Dutch settlers named the plant *kraanbere*, from which the English word is derived.

The tart fruit ripens in the fall and is harvested by flooding the bog with about 16 inches of water. A water paddle then churns the water to loosen the berries from the vines, after which they float to the top. The berries are then corralled into one corner of the bog using wooden booms, a process that creates a crimson half-moon at the edge of the pond. This stage of the harvesting is one of the most colorful fall scenes on the Cape and Islands. After the booming, the berries are scooped up and shipped off to make cranberry juice and sauce.

The trail at Windswept Cranberry Bog goes through the center of the property, passing alongside cranberry bogs and marshland. It then crosses an earthen dike on the edge of Stump Pond and makes a small loop through an old hardwood forest before returning back along the same route. This is an easy trail that is enjoyable at any time of year and usually offers a glimpse of wildlife. Cottontail rabbits and ducks are particularly abundant. If you should happen to walk this trail in winter, you'll likely find the bogs flooded and iced over. When water freezes on the bog, the ice, which remains at 32 degrees Fahrenheit, acts as an insulator, protecting the plants from subfreezing temperatures and blustery winds.

Access

From the town of Nantucket, go east on Orange Street until you reach the rotary, where you then take Milestone Road as if heading toward Siasconset. Shortly past the rotary, turn left onto Polpis Road. Continue 4.8 miles on Polpis Road, then turn right into the Windswept Cranberry Bog parking lot. This property, like other Nantucket Conservation Foundation holdings, is posted with boundary markers that depict the foundation's logo of a gull and waves.

Trail

The trail leads south from the parking lot along a dirt service road and, after a few hundred yards, enters an open area of cranberry bogs. During the first 5 minutes, you'll pass four tiny service roads that branch off to the right and skirt the bogs before reaching a major fork, where you'll turn right. At this point, you can see woods ahead and a lone pine tree at the right side of the trail.

When the road begins to curve right around the south side of the bog, take the grassy track straight up the hill along the edge of a thicket. The path then enters a shrubby area where panic grass, winterberry, arrowwood, groundsel tree, milkweed, grapevines, and highbush blueberries grow.

In a few minutes, the trail curves to the right, and you'll come to a dike that runs along the northwestern edge of Stump Pond. The stumps sticking up out of the shallow water bear witness to the fact that this is not a natural pond, but an artificial reservoir created to feed water to the bogs. The pond is a special place, with an almost haunting beauty. It provides habitat for black ducks, mallards, and black-crowned night herons and serves as a watering spot for white-tailed deer.

After crossing the dike, the trail leads into a mixed hardwood forest with oak, red maple, sassafras, and tupelo trees. Almost immediately, the trail splits in three. Continue straight ahead, on the middle trail, to begin a small loop. After a few minutes, you will reach another dike at the side of a small pond, but instead of crossing the dike, turn right. This section of the trail is damp and shady, bordering a swampy marsh on the left. You'll pass some of Nantucket's largest holly trees before coming to some grand old American beech trees with curling limbs. Shortly after these stately trees, the trail completes the loop. Turn left, recross the Stump Pond dike, and return to the parking lot on the same trail you came in on.

Appendix

Environmental Organizations

The following environmental groups are active in land preservation efforts on Cape Cod, Martha's Vineyard, and Nantucket. Many of them provide brochures with information on properties under their jurisdictions.

Barnstable Conservation
  Commission
Barnstable Town Hall
367 Main Street
Hyannis, MA 02601
508-790-6245

Bourne Conservation
  Commission
Bourne Town Hall
24 Perry Avenue
Bourne, MA 02532
508-759-6025

Bourne Conservation Trust
PO Box 203
Cataumet, MA 02534

Brewster Conservation
  Commission
Brewster Town Hall
2198 Main Street
Brewster, MA 02536
508-896-3701, ext. 35

Cape Cod National Seashore
  Administration Office
PO Box 250
South Wellfleet, MA 02663
508-255-3785

Cape Cod Pathways Cape Cod
  Commission
3225 Main Street
Barnstable, MA 02630
508-362-3828

Dennis Conservation Department
Dennis Town Hall
PO Box 1419
485 Main Street
South Dennis, MA 02660
508-760-6123

Falmouth Conservation
  Commission
59 Town Hall Square
Falmouth, MA 02540
508-548-7611

Friends of the Mashpee
  National Wildlife Refuge
PO Box 1283
Mashpee, MA 02649
508-495-1702

Martha's Vineyard Land Bank
  Commission
PO Box 2057
Edgartown, MA 02539
508-627-7141

Mashpee Conservation
  Commission
16 Great Neck Road North
Mashpee, MA 02649
508-539-1414

Massachusetts Audubon Society
Wellfleet Bay Wildlife Sanctuary
PO Box 236
South Wellfleet, MA 02663
508-349-2615

Nantucket Conservation
  Foundation
PO Box 13
118 Cliff Road
Nantucket, MA 02554
508-288-2884

Nantucket Land Bank
22 Broad Street
Nantucket, MA 02554
508-228-7240

Orleans Conservation
  Commission
Orleans Town Offices
Orleans, MA 02653
508-240-3700, ext. 425

Sandwich Conservation
  Commission
16 Jan Sebastian Drive
Sandwich, MA 02563
508-888-4200

Sheriff's Meadow Foundation
  Mary P. Wakeman
  Conservation Center
RR1, Box 319X
Vineyard Haven, MA 02568
508-693-5207

Waquoit Bay National Estuarine
  Research Reserve
PO Box 3092
Route 28
Waquoit, MA 02536
508-457-0495

Yarmouth Conservation
  Commission
Yarmouth Town Hall
1146 Route 28
South Yarmouth, MA 02664
508-398-2231, ext. 283

Suggested Reading

Alden, Peter, and Brian Cassie. *National Audubon Society Field Guide to New England.* New York: Alfred A. Knopf, 1998.

Baisly, Clair. *Cape Cod Architecture.* Hyannis, Mass.: Parnassus Imprints, 1989.

Beston, Henry. *The Outermost House.* New York: Henry Holt and Company, 1929.

Cape Cod Bird Club & Massachusetts Audubon Society. *Birding Cape Cod.* Massachusetts Audubon Society, 1994.

Clark, Admont G. *Lighthouses of Cape Cod–Martha's Vineyard–Nantucket.* Hyannis, Mass.: Parnassus Imprints, 1992.

Dalton, J.W. *The Life Savers of Cape Cod.* Originally published in 1902. Hyannis, Mass.: Parnassus Imprints, 1991.

Davidson, Donald W. *America's Landfall: The Historic Lighthouses of Cape Cod, Nantucket & Martha's Vineyard.* Cape Cod, Mass.: The Peninsula Press, 1996.

DiGregorio, Mario, and Jeff Wallner. *A Vanishing Heritage: Wildflowers of Cape Cod.* Missoula, Mont.: Mountain Press Publishing Company, 1989.

Dunford, Fred, and Greg O'Brien. *Secrets in the Sand: The Archaeology of Cape Cod.* Hyannis, Mass.: Parnassus Imprints, 1997.

Finch, Robert. *The Cape Itself.* New York: W. W. Norton & Company, 1991.

Forman, H. Chandler. *Early Nantucket and Its Whale Houses.* Nantucket, Mass.: Mill Hill Press, 1991.

Grant, Kimberly. *Cape Cod: An Explorer's Guide,* Third Edition. Woodstock, Vt.: The Countryman Press, 1999.

Hale, Anne. *Moraine to Marsh: A Field Guide to Martha's Vineyard.* Vineyard Haven, Mass.: Watership Gardens, 1988.

Kittredge, Henry C. *Cape Cod: Its People and Their History.* Hyannis, Mass.: Parnassus Imprints, 1995.

Leach, Robert J., and Peter Gow. *Quaker Nantucket.* Nantucket, Mass.: Mill Hill Press, 1997.

Meigs, Frances B. *My Grandfather, Thornton W. Burgess.* Beverly, Mass.: Commonwealth Editions, 1998.

Melville, Herman. *Moby-Dick.* Originally published in 1851. Random House.

Merrill, Christopher. *The Way to the Salt Marsh: A John Hay Reader.* Hanover, N.H.: University Press of New England, 1998.

Milton, Susan, and Kevin and Nan Jeffrey. *25 Bicycle Tours on Cape Cod and the Islands.* Woodstock, Vt.: The Countryman Press, 1996.

Mulloney, Stephen. *Traces of Thoreau.* Boston: Northeastern University Press, 1998.

Niering, William A., and Nancy Olmstead. The *Audubon Society Field Guide to North American Wildflowers: Eastern Region.* New York: Alfred A. Knopf, 1979.

O'Brien, Greg. *A Guide to Nature on Cape Cod and the Islands.* Hyannis, Mass.: Parnassus Imprints, 1995.

Oldale, Robert N. *Cape Cod and the Islands: The Geologic Story.* Hyannis, Mass.: Parnassus Imprints, 1992.

Petrides, George A., and Janet Wehr. *Peterson Field Guide: Eastern Trees.* Boston: Houghton Mifflin, 1988.

Philbrick, Nathaniel. *Away Offshore, Nantucket Island and Its People, 1602–1890.* Nantucket, Mass.: Mill Hill Press, 1994.

Quinn, William P. *Cape Cod Maritime Disasters.* Orleans, Mass.: Lower Cape Publishing, 1990.

Richardson, Wyman. *The House on Nauset Marsh.* Woodstock, Vt.: The Countryman Press, 1997.

Schuler, Stanley. *Saltbox and Cape Cod Houses.* West Chester, Pa.: Schiffer Publishing, 1988.

Strahler, Arthur N. *A Geologist's View of Cape Cod.* Hyannis, Mass.: Parnassus Imprints, 1966.

Thoreau, Henry David. *Cape Cod.* Originally published 1864. Hyannis, Mass.: Parnassus Imprints, 1997.

Let Backcountry Guides Take You There

Our experienced backcountry authors will lead you to the finest trails, parks, and back roads in the following areas:

50 Hikes Series

50 Hikes in the Maine Mountains
50 Hikes in Southern and Coastal Maine
50 Hikes in Vermont
50 Hikes in the White Mountains
50 More Hikes in New Hampshire
50 Hikes in Connecticut
50 Hikes in Massachusetts
50 Hikes in the Hudson Valley
50 Hikes in the Adirondacks
50 Hikes in Central New York
50 Hikes in Western New York
50 Hikes in New Jersey
50 Hikes in Eastern Pennsylvania
50 Hikes in Central Pennsylvania
50 Hikes in Western Pennsylvania
50 Hikes in the Mountains of North
    Carolina
50 Hikes in Northern Virginia
50 Hikes in Ohio
50 Hikes in Michigan

Walks and Rambles Series

Walks and Rambles on Cape Cod and
    the Islands
Walks and Rambles in Rhode Island
More Walks and Rambles in Rhode
    Island
Walks and Rambles on the Delmarva
    Peninsula
Walks and Rambles in Southwestern
    Ohio
Walks and Rambles in Ohio's Western
    Reserve
Walks and Rambles in the Western
    Hudson Valley
Walks and Rambles on Long Island

25 Bicycle Tours Series

25 Bicycle Tours in Maine
30 Bicycle Tours in New Hampshire
25 Bicycle Tours in Vermont
25 Mountain Bike Tours in Vermont
25 Bicycle Tours on Cape Cod and the
    Islands
25 Mountain Bike Tours in Massachusetts
30 Bicycle Tours in New Jersey
25 Mountain Bike Tours in New Jersey
25 Bicycle Tours in the Adirondacks
30 Bicycle Tours in the Finger Lakes
    Region
25 Bicycle Tours in the Hudson Valley
25 Bicycle Tours in the Twin Cities and
    Southeastern Minnesota
30 Bicycle Tours in Wisconsin
25 Mountain Bike Tours in the
    Hudson Valley
25 Bicycle Tours in Ohio's
    Western Reserve
25 Bicycle Tours in Maryland
25 Bicycle Tours on Delmarva
25 Bicycle Tours in and around
    Washington, D.C.
25 Bicycle Tours in Coastal Georgia and
    the Carolina Low Country
25 Bicycle Tours in the Texas Hill Country
    and West Texas

We offer many more books on hiking, fly-fishing, travel, nature, and other subjects. Our books are available at bookstores and outdoor stores everywhere. For more information or a free catalog, please call 1-800-245-4151 or write to us at The Countryman Press, PO Box 748, Woodstock, Vermont 05091. You can find us on the web at www.countrymanpress.com